W9-CFR-342

First published March, 2006 by

WORLD CLASS COACHING 15004 Buena Vista Drive, Leawood, KS 66224 (913) 402-0030

ISBN 0-9773419-2-5

Author – David Wall
Edited by Mike Saif

Cover by John Babcock, Illustration & Design

Published by

WORLD CLASS COACHING

INTRODUCTION

This book deals with player's roles and responsibilities within different systems of play. It covers both the attacking and defending duties of each player. All formations (systems of play) are covered including the 4-4-2, 4-3-3, 3-4-3, 3-5-2, etc.

So whether your team plays with four or three defenders; three, four or five midfielders or one, two or three forwards, this book will show you in detail the responsibilities for each of those players.

This book is an ideal training guide for players and coaches. It will enhance your overall knowledge of the various systems of play. It will also help the player's understanding of what is expected from them within the team.

Also included are specific drills and game related activities you can use in your training sessions to help your players train for their specific position.

Table of Contents

Introduction

Movement of the player

Movement of the Ball

Player

Cones used as goals
 in training activities

Cones used as players
starting position
in midfield training activities

Target Area for players to run to

Playing field

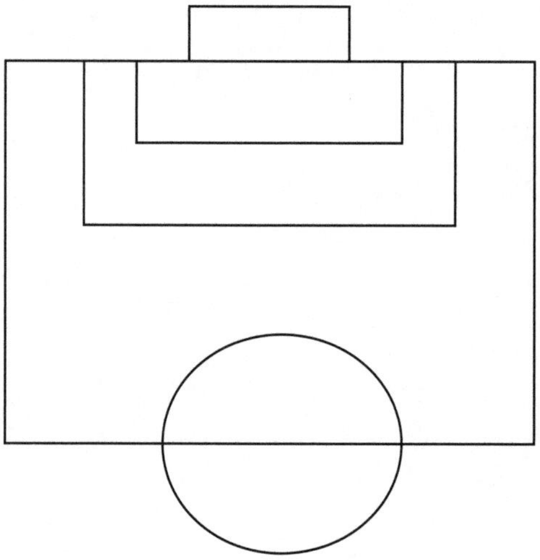

"Dedication"

To my late mother Eileen Wall whose courage and strength through years of illness have been an inspiration to my life and to my father James and brother Andrew for all there encouragement throughout my career.

"Acknowledgements"

Steve Round
Rob Straw
John Tudor
Wayne Harrison
Tonka United Soccer Association

Chapter 1

Selecting your players

Selecting your players

- **Pre - season**

At the beginning of each season at professional, amateur and youth levels, you the coach and coaching staff at your club are busy searching, marketing, identifying and recruiting players to either

(a) Come and tryout for your team

(b) You as a coach have identified them and have previous knowledge on the recruited player and you offer them a place on your team.

One way or another, coaches all around the world at all levels are trying to promote and improve there squad of players for the upcoming season.

Before the season starts the coach should have a certain vision on how you would like to play and how you would like to mold you're team together, however keep in mind that you may need to adjust things as your season goes along adapting to your players needs and various situations that may arise. So choosing your players with your vision in mind becomes a key ingredient to selecting and defining your team.

- **What do I need to look for in a player?**

The main component is does the player have a good understanding of the game.

Can he or she solve problems within the context of the game in a positional role?

Positional roles are broken into 4 area's Goalkeepers, Defenders, Midfield, and Forward's.

Whilst assessing your players through the evaluation process of games practices and testing formats, keep in mind that some players may have the ability to play in other positions and may not be restricted to just playing in a certain position. Other factors that can influence your decisions are.

- A player may perform <u>well in a testing environment</u> but may not be able to carry it over to the game environment.

- A player may be able to perform <u>well in a game environment</u> but may not test well.

Added to that, there are the physical, technical, tactical, and psychological abilities of a player to be taken into consideration.

"What are the ideal qualities needed in a player."

- **Physical Fitness:**

Good Size and Strength: will help players with the demands of the game.

Good Speed and Quickness: The ability to separate your-self and get away from opponents quickly over short and long distances is a big advantage both with and without the ball.

Reaction Speed to both the player and the ball.

Good Aerobic endurance: Players having the ability to play through the duration of a game.

Good Anaerobic base: During games players will not only have to run for longer periods but will also have to cover short distances at various levels of speed , being able to adjust and recover quickly within the game is vital.

Good Agility , Balance, and Coordination,: During games players will have many challenges, jogging , running, sprinting ,tackling , bending , jumping , sharp changes of direction, sometimes with a ball and sometimes without a ball .

Good Communicational Skill's: Talking to your team-mates, providing good information during game and practices.

- **Technique**

Passing and Shooting: A good variety of passing and shooting technique's, with the inside / outside of both feet, striking the ball smoothly with good accuracy and range.

Receiving: Having a good 1st touch under pressure with various surfaces of the body (Feet, Thighs, Chest, Head) <u>For Goalkeepers in addition to having these qualities they will also need to have good safe hands.</u>

Dribbling and Turning: Good control while dribbling at speed with both feet and a good variety of attacking moves, fakes, feints ,also being able to shield and possess the ball using various turning techniques such as pull backs , inside and outside cuts , cryuff turns , and step over's.

Heading: Whether you are attacking or defending, having the attitude and ability to time the flight of the ball and use the correct surface to head the ball is a vital component of the game especially when teams attack through the air, for example dealing with corner kicks.

- **Technique under pressure:**

Whilst being able to control, pass and shoot, can a player perform those tasks under the pressures of the game environment, both having the confidence and composure on the ball, yet also dealing with opposition, and the ability to perform those tasks when a player is physically and mentally tired?

9

- **Tactical Awareness:**

Positional sense, does the player understand and have good knowledge of the requirements needed when playing in there position, both when your team is attacking and when your team is defending. Does the player posses defending qualities or attacking qualities or do they have both.

Having good vision before they receive the ball and when the have the ball, does the player have craft and imagination, players who can show these qualities are ideal for your team.

And lastly is the player flexible, can they play in different positions.

- **Psychological:**

Confidence and Composure, when a player has confidence and self belief in there own ability, That player will grow and your team will benefit with there presence, however every player at some stage will have to deal with adversity both on and off the field, how they handle that pressure and how you as a coach deal with those pressures are the key to peak performance. Players who are strong mentally will be able to deal with adversity better than others.

Finally

"Can the player deal with and impact the designated level of play on a consistent basis".

Although these are the ideal qualities needed in a player for a certain role, the majority of players may be limited to a couple of these requirements.

For Example some forwards are not quick but have the ability to score goals. Some midfield players lack size and strength but have good distribution skills. Some defenders are not as good on the ball, but show strength, size and the ability to lead a team by example.

All need to be woven together to mould and create the team.

"Evaluation Process"

During this process it can be a very exciting time for the coach but also very stressful as well.

With most evaluation processes each club or team will have its own format and criteria Evaluation format's usually consist of:

1. skills and fitness assessments:
2. small sided games assessments
3. full sided games assessments
4. A combination of the above.

For the coach this is usually the most exciting time as you get to see your returning players from the previous season and then get a good look at the new players coming in. After evaluations and your information are collected you will have a good idea on the strengths and weakness of each player and whether or not you would like them in your team.

- **Making your decisions and molding your team:**

This can be a stressful time for the coach as major decisions are made for the upcoming season on player personnel.

Some considerations to be taken into account when making these decisions are:

- What is the coaches vision?
- How many players do I need in my squad?
- How many goalkeepers do I take?
- How many defenders do I take?
- How many midfield players do I take?
- How many strikers do i take?
- Do I have any players that are currently injured that I want to include?
- Rules of the Association or league, can i replace players throughout the season or is my roster restricted once my team is picked.
- Will this player be good for our team chemistry?
- How am I going to address communicating to players / players parents that they did not make the squad?

Not only is it a stressful time for coaches but also for players as well , especially youth players, you will have some tough decisions to make, For those players who make the team it is a great feeling , however for those who don't it can be a stressful experience. Unfortunately there is no easy way of telling players that they did not make the team.

Once you have made all your decisions, it is then time to start molding your squad together introducing your new players, organizing and implementing your ideas and look forward to your season.

Chapter 2
Getting to know your players

Getting to know your players

Once you have selected your players, developing a relationship between coach and player is an important stage of the development for both the individual and the squad.
Creating chemistry and cohesion within your team takes time, so it is important at the beginning of each season to set the tone of expectations, rules and philosophies for both players and coaches.
Practicing and playing together will help over time; however you as a coach can help with the development of your squad from the 1st day you get together.
By establishing these basic principles between coach's and players, even parents if you are involved in youth levels you will help everyone learn and grow through the experience.

Developing chemistry and cohesion within your squad:
Considerations to take into account are:
- Age of your players
- Gender of your players
- Playing abilities and level of your players.

Setting the tone <u>off</u> the field:
Considerations to take into account are:

• Player meetings at practices / games	Individual / Group / Team
• Player questionnaires	
• Team meetings	Setting Goal's , Expectations, Rules
	Players / Coach's
	Individual / Team
• Social Events	Team Oriented
• Travel	Taking your team away
	Team Bonding

Setting the tone <u>on</u> the field as a coach:
Considerations to take into account:

• Appearance	Look like a Coach
• Demeanor	Positive
• Attitude	Positive
• Enthusiasm	Players will feed of your enthusiasm
• Your communication	Simple Clear and Concise
• Being organized	Preparation
• Training environment	Providing a safe and structured environment
• Playing environment	Observing

Training environment:

Although a lot of the time the focus will be implementing and improving on a style of play and system of play for the team, working with your individual players on there strengths and weakness should not be overlooked.

For your team to improve your players will need to improve, by setting aside time within your training structure to work with them will help your players with there own personnel goals.

This is done through working with observing them play in game and training environments on a weekly basis.

There are many different ways to record and track player's statistics, however you as the coach of the team will have your opinion on what they need to work on. It is important to continue the growth of the player's strengths as well as identifying and working on there weakness. Through functional training activities that are specific to the needs and role of the positions, the players will be able to not only improve on there technical abilities but also will improve there knowledge and understanding of the position you want them to play.

Communication and feedback between the coach and the player throughout the season is vital for continued personnel and team growth.

Player Evaluation / Review
Strength's and weakness

*Player Name:*_____ *Age :*_____

*Coach Name:*_____

*Team:*_____

*Players Preferred Position:*_____

*Date:*_____

Points System:
5 = Excellent, 4 = Above Average, 3 = Average, 2 = Below Average, 1 = Needs Development

Characteristics		*Comments*
Appearance	5 4 3 2 1	
Application during the game	5 4 3 2 1	
Attendance, Practice	5 4 3 2 1	
Attendance, Games	5 4 3 2 1	
Willingness to Learn Concentration	5 4 3 2 1	
Attitude in: Practice	5 4 3 2 1	
Games	5 4 3 2 1	
Communication Skills	5 4 3 2 1	

Physical Characteristics		Comments
Physical size & presence *(Ability to compete)*	5 4 3 2 1	
Strength *On the Ball*	5 4 3 2 1	
Endurance Aerobic *(Ability to play for long periods in Games)*	5 4 3 2 1	
Speed and Pace Anaerobic *Short Sprints* *Long Sprints*	5 4 3 2 1 5 4 3 2 1	
Agility **Flexibility of movement** **Coordination**	5 4 3 2 1 5 4 3 2 1 5 4 3 2 1	

Technical Ability		Comments
Passing *Accuracy.* *Range.* *Weight.* *The ability to use both feet.*	*5 4 3 2 1* *5 4 3 2 1* *5 4 3 2 1* *5 4 3 2 1*	
Receiving *Quality of 1st touch* *Without pressure* *Under Pressure* *Retaining possession*	*5 4 3 2 1* *5 4 3 2 1* *5 4 3 2 1*	
Turning with the ball *Ability to change the angle of the ball using a specific turn* *Inside cut* *Outside cut* *Pull back* *Other*	*5 4 3 2 1* *5 4 3 2 1* *5 4 3 2 1* *5 4 3 2 1*	
Dribbling *Ability to use disguise to beat defenders in tight areas* *Fast footwork moves* *Body Fakes/Feints*	*5 4 3 2 1* *5 4 3 2 1*	
Running with the Ball *Ability to run the ball into space playing at speed.*	*5 4 3 2 1*	
Shooting and Finishing *Ability to get shots on Target and Score*	*5 4 3 2 1*	
Heading *Willingness to head the ball*	*5 4 3 2 1*	

Tactical Application		Comments
Impact on the game	5 4 3 2 1	
Knowledge of positional role on the field	5 4 3 2 1	
Decisions Making		
On the ball	5 4 3 2 1	
Off the ball	5 4 3 2 1	
Goalkeeping		
Technical Hands / Feet With no pressure	5 4 3 2 1	
Under pressure	5 4 3 2 1	
Distribution Goal-kicks	5 4 3 2 1	
Kicking out of hands	5 4 3 2 1	
Throwing	5 4 3 2 1	
Tactical Decision Making	5 4 3 2 1	
Organizational skills (Set Plays)	5 4 3 2 1	
Communicational Skills	5 4 3 2 1	
Dealing with shots	5 4 3 2 1	
Dealing with crosses	5 4 3 2 1	
Dealing with back passes	5 4 3 2 1	

Chapter 3
Selecting a system of play
to suit your players

Selecting a system to suit your players

Once you have selected your players and got to know there individual strengths and weaknesses, the ultimate question is:

"WHAT SYSTEM SHALL WE USE AND HOW ARE WE GOING TO PLAY?"

There are many systems of play to choose from 4-4-2, 4-3-3, 3-5-2, 3-4-3 etc
Playing a certain system is NOT the magical answer to winning soccer games as which ever system of play you use; the system is only as good as the players you have in your team.
Consequently there are strengths and weakness within your players as well as the system of play you are implementing.
When selecting a system of play here are some considerations to take into account.
*   The overall ability of your players (age, gender, fitness levels)
*   The players knowledge of there responsibilities within the system.
*   The opposition and how they play.
As a coach it is important that you to have a good understanding on the principles of the game, knowledge of the specific system you want to play, how it works, and how you want to implement it, to your players. Over time, by implementing your ideas, through practices and games, your team, will develop a style of play that allows your players to express themselves to the best of there ability.
Keep in mind that, <u>your expectations</u> on how you want to play <u>need to be realistic</u> in relation to the ability and limitations of your players.
A system of play and style of play must fit with the abilities and characteristics of your players
Organizing your players within the system of play:
Considerations:
*   Players should be placed in a positional role based on there playing strengths
For example players who show good attacking and defending tendencies may fit into a midfield role
Players who show good defending qualities may fit into a defending role at the back.
Players who show good attacking qualities and scores goals but has poor defending qualities may fit in as a striker's role.
*   You can ask your players where they are most comfortable playing.
Some players will also communicate to you where they feel there best position is on the field.
*   Selecting a players position based on there technical ability.
For example placing players who predominately play with there left foot on the left side and players who play predominantly with there right foot on the right side.
Players who are naturally both footed may play in central role.
*   As a coach you may see some qualities in a player for a certain role that the player has never played before, how you approach the player and getting them to believe in your decision is the key to the player being successful in that role.
*   Being adaptable, if you feel you need to change your system of play for the good of your players, do so however communication to your players is vital.

- Style of Play
  Do we play direct ?
  Do we build up out of the defending 1/3rd ?
  Do we play a combination of both ?

  Again the abilities of your players and your expectations are the key to success when developing a style of play.

Chapter 4
Player's role and responsibilities
in a 4-4-2 system of play

Introduction

The following presentation is a guide for coaches and players to enable them to better understand the specific positions and demands of the game within a 4 – 4 – 2 playing formation a 4-3-3 playing formation and a 3-5-2 playing formation.

There are 3 key areas in the game where players have major responsibilities.

1. Their role when defending.
2. Their role when attacking.
3. Their awareness in transition between attacking and defending.

In addition to these responsibilities.

There are 4 key components within a player that need to be considered.

1. The physical ability of a player
2. The technical ability of a player
3. The tactical awareness of a player
4. The psychological make up of a player.

The 1st part looks at player responsibilities in a 4-4-2 formation.

The 4 specific areas on the field where we need to accommodate players in a 4-4-2 formation are.

1. Goalkeeper
2. 4 Defenders
3. 4 Midfield players
4. 2 Forwards

The 2nd part deals with player responsibilities in a 4-3-3 playing formation:

The 4 specific areas on the field where we need to accommodate players in a 4-3-3 formation are.

1. Goalkeeper
2. 4 Defenders
3. 3 Midfield players
4. 3 Forwards

The 3rd part deals with player responsibilities in a 3-5-2 playing formation:

The 4 specific areas on the field where we need to accommodate players in a 4-3-3 formation are.

1. Goalkeeper
2. 3 Defenders
3. 5 Midfield players
4. 2 Forwards

Playing Roles in a 4 - 4 - 2 formation
Goalkeeper

<table>
<tr><td>

Role in Defense:
- Good Communication.
- Command your 6 yard / 18 yard box.
- Last line of defense.
- Stop the ball from shots and crosses.
- Provide **Cover / Balance** to the back 4 defenders.

</td><td>

Role in Attack:
- Good Communication.
- 1st line of attack.
- Quality distribution to Defenders / Midfield / Forward Players.
- Provide **Support** to defenders / midfield.

</td></tr>
</table>

← *Transition* →

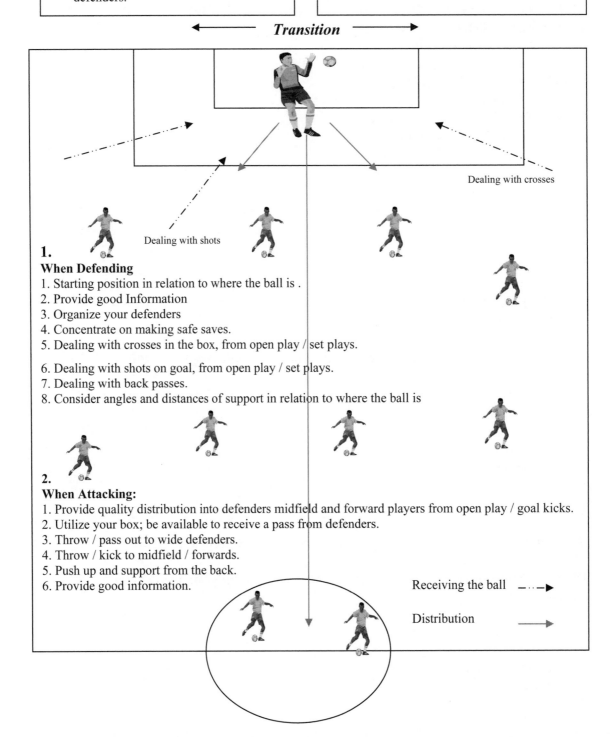

Dealing with crosses

Dealing with shots

1.

When Defending

1. Starting position in relation to where the ball is .
2. Provide good Information
3. Organize your defenders
4. Concentrate on making safe saves.
5. Dealing with crosses in the box, from open play / set plays.

6. Dealing with shots on goal, from open play / set plays.
7. Dealing with back passes.
8. Consider angles and distances of support in relation to where the ball is

2.

When Attacking:

1. Provide quality distribution into defenders midfield and forward players from open play / goal kicks.
2. Utilize your box; be available to receive a pass from defenders.
3. Throw / pass out to wide defenders.
4. Throw / kick to midfield / forwards.
5. Push up and support from the back.
6. Provide good information.

Receiving the ball ‐ · · ‐▶

Distribution ─────▶

Playing Roles Right Defender
4 – 4 – 2 Formation

<table>
<tr><td>

Role in Defense:
- Good communication.
- Mark attackers as directed / zonal man to man.
- Provide **Pressure** and **Support** when play is on right side of the field.
- Provide **Cover** and **Balance** when Ball is on opposite side of the field.

</td><td>

Role in Attack:
- Good communication.
- Be available to receive a pass, **Width / Depth.**
- Quality **Distribution** to midfield / forward players.
- Provide **Support** to defenders / midfield / forwards with good movement off the ball.

</td></tr>
</table>

← *Transition* →

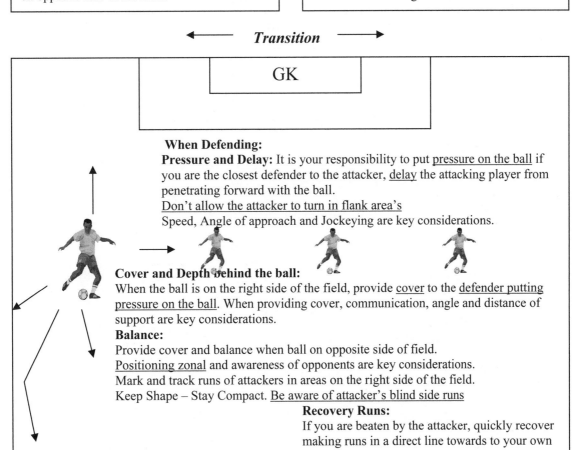

GK

When Defending:

Pressure and Delay: It is your responsibility to put <u>pressure on the ball</u> if you are the closest defender to the attacker, <u>delay</u> the attacking player from penetrating forward with the ball.
<u>Don't allow the attacker to turn in flank area's</u>
Speed, Angle of approach and Jockeying are key considerations.

Cover and Depth behind the ball:
When the ball is on the right side of the field, provide <u>cover</u> to the <u>defender putting pressure on the ball</u>. When providing cover, communication, angle and distance of support are key considerations.

Balance:
Provide cover and balance when ball on opposite side of field.
<u>Positioning zonal</u> and awareness of opponents are key considerations.
Mark and track runs of attackers in areas on the right side of the field.
Keep Shape – Stay Compact. <u>Be aware of attacker's blind side runs</u>

Recovery Runs:
If you are beaten by the attacker, quickly recover making runs in a direct line towards to your own goal.

2. When Attacking:

Penetration, When you win the ball, in transition, can you go forward, by either <u>passing, running with the ball</u>. <u>Provide quality distribution</u> to defenders, midfield players and forwards, short passes, driven passes and long- lofted passes down the line, or diagonal passes to switch play.
<u>Also support passes to goalkeeper</u>
If in a position in and around opponent's penalty area, can you shoot to score or get crosses into the penalty box.

Width and Depth:
Provide width and depth by identifying and <u>moving into spaces off the ball</u> in front or behind the player with the ball, Be available at all times to receive a pass. This will help stretch opponents defensive shape.

Mobility: Provide good movement off the ball, <u>Overlapping runs</u> into forward areas, when possible

Playing Roles Left Defender
4 – 4 – 2 Formation

<table>
<tr><td>

Role in Defense:
- Good communication.
- Mark attackers as directed zonal, man to man.
- Provide **Pressure** and **Support** when play is on the left side of the field.
- Provide **Cover** and **Balance** when ball is on opposite side of the field.

</td><td>

Role in Attack:
- Good communication.
- Be available to receive a pass, **Width Depth.**
- Quality **Distribution** to midfield / forward player.
- Provide **Support** to defenders / midfield / forwards with good movement off the ball.

</td></tr>
</table>

← *Transition* →

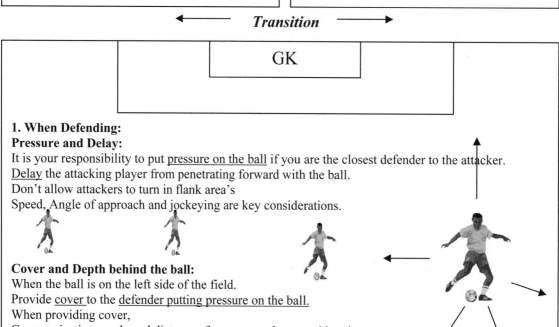

GK

1. When Defending:
Pressure and Delay:
It is your responsibility to put <u>pressure on the ball</u> if you are the closest defender to the attacker.
<u>Delay</u> the attacking player from penetrating forward with the ball.
Don't allow attackers to turn in flank area's
Speed, Angle of approach and jockeying are key considerations.

Cover and Depth behind the ball:
When the ball is on the left side of the field.
Provide <u>cover</u> to the <u>defender putting pressure on the ball.</u>
When providing cover,
Communication, angle and distance of support are key considerations.
Balance:
Provide cover and balance when ball on opposite side of field.
<u>Positioning zonal</u> and awareness of opponents are key considerations.
Mark and track runs of attackers in areas on the left side of the field.
Keep Shape – Stay Compact. <u>Be aware of attacker's blind side runs</u>
Recovery Runs:
If you are beaten by the attacker, quickly recover making runs in a direct line towards to your own goal.

2.When Attacking:
Penetration, When you win the ball, in transition, can you go forward.
by either <u>passing, running with the ball</u>
<u>Provide quality distribution</u> to defenders, midfield players and forwards, short passes, driven passes and long- lofted passes down the line, or diagonal passes to switch play. <u>Also support passes to goalkeeper</u>
If in a position in and around opponent's penalty area, can you shoot to score or get a cross in the box.
Width and Depth
Provide width and depth by identifying <u>and moving into spaces off the ball</u> in front or behind the player with the ball, Be available at all times to receive a pass. This will help stretch opponents defensive shape.
Mobility: Provide good movement off the ball, <u>Overlapping runs</u> into forward areas when possible

Playing Roles Central Defender (Right Side)
4 – 4 – 2 Formation

<table>
<tr>
<td>

Role in Defense:
- Good communication.
- Mark attackers as directed, zonal, man to man.
- Provide **Pressure** and support when play is in central areas of the field.
- Provide **Cover** and **Balance** when ball is in flank areas of the field.

</td>
<td>

Role in Attack:
- Good communication.
- Be available to receive a pass, **Width / Depth.**
- Quality **Distribution** to midfield / forward players.
- Provide **Support** to defenders / midfield players and forwards.

</td>
</tr>
</table>

← *Transition* →

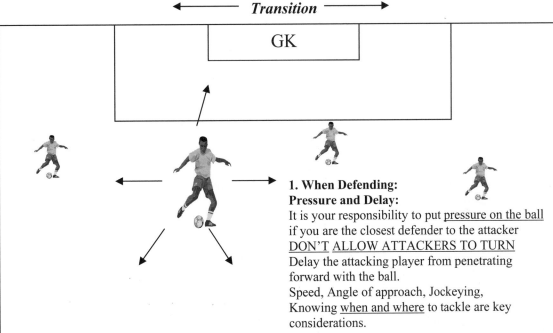

GK

1. When Defending:
Pressure and Delay:
It is your responsibility to put <u>pressure on the ball</u> if you are the closest defender to the attacker <u>DON'T ALLOW ATTACKERS TO TURN</u>
Delay the attacking player from penetrating forward with the ball.
Speed, Angle of approach, Jockeying, Knowing <u>when and where</u> to tackle are key considerations.

Cover and Depth behind the ball:
When the ball is on your side of the field, provide <u>cover</u> to your teammate who is putting pressure on the ball. When providing cover, communication, angle and distance of support are key considerations.
Balance:
Provide cover and balance when ball is in wide areas of field.
Positioning either <u>zonal / man to man</u>, awareness of opponent's positions are key considerations.
Mark and track runs of attackers in central areas of the field.
Keep Shape – Stay Compact, Good Communication needed.
Form partnership with other central defender, right defender.
Recovery Runs: If you are beaten by the attacker, quickly recover making runs in a direct line towards to your own goal.
2. When Attacking:
Penetration, When you win the ball, in transition, can you go forward, by either passing, or running the ball out of defense?
<u>Provide quality distribution</u> to outside defenders, midfield players and forwards, short passes, driven passes and long- lofted passes to start the attack. <u>Also support passes to goalkeeper</u>.
Depth Provide depth by identifying and moving into spaces off the ball, distance and angle of support behind the player with the ball are key considerations
Be available at all times to receive a pass.
Mobility <u>Provide good movement off the ball in a supporting role</u>

Playing Roles Central Defender (Left Side)
4 – 4 – 2 Formation

<table>
<tr><td>

Role in Defense:
- Good communication.
- Mark attackers as directed, zonal, man to man
- **Pressure** and support when play is central areas of the field.
- **Cover and Balance** when ball is on wide areas of the field.

</td><td>

Role in Attack:
- Good communication.
- Be available to receive a pass , **Width / Depth**
- Quality **Distribution** to midfield / forward players.
- Provide **Support** to defenders / midfield / forwards.

</td></tr>
</table>

Transition ←——————→

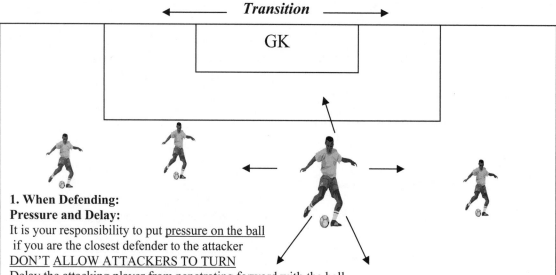

GK

1. When Defending:

Pressure and Delay:
It is your responsibility to put <u>pressure on the ball</u>
if you are the closest defender to the attacker
<u>DON'T ALLOW ATTACKERS TO TURN</u>
Delay the attacking player from penetrating forward with the ball.
Speed, Angle of approach, Jockeying,
Knowing <u>when and where</u> to tackle are key considerations.

Cover and Depth behind the ball:
When the ball is on your side of the field, provide cover to your teammate who is putting pressure on the ball. When providing cover, communication, angle and distance of support are key considerations.

Balance:
Provide cover and balance when ball is in wide areas of field.
Positioning either zonal / man to man, awareness of opponent's positions are key considerations.
Mark and track runs of attackers in central areas of the field.
Keep Shape – Stay Compact, Good Communication needed.
Form partnership with other central defender, left defender.

Recovery Runs:
If you are beaten by the attacker, quickly recover making runs in a direct line towards to your own goal.

2.When Attacking:

Penetration: When you win the ball, in transition, can you go forward, by either <u>passing</u>, or <u>running</u> the ball out of defense?
<u>Provide quality distribution</u> to outside defenders, midfield players and forwards, <u>short passes</u>, <u>driven passes</u> and <u>long- lofted passes</u> to start the attack. <u>Also support passes to goalkeeper</u>

Depth: Provide depth by identifying and moving into spaces off the ball, distance and angle of support behind the player with the ball are key considerations, be available at all times to receive a pass.

Mobility: <u>Provide good movement off the ball in a supporting role.</u>

Playing Roles Central Midfield (Holding)
4 – 4 – 2 Formation

<table>
<tr><td>

Role in Defense:
- Good communication.
- Marking and tracking opponents in central areas of the field.
- **Pressure** on the ball and support your midfield / defenders. when play is in central areas of the field.
- **Cover and Balance** when ball on opposite sides of the field.

</td><td>

Role in Attack:
- Good communication.
- Be available to receive a pass.
- Quality **Distribution** to defenders / midfield / forward players.
- **Support** to defenders / midfield / forwards with good movement off the ball - **Mobility**

</td></tr>
</table>

← *Transition* →

```
                    GK
```

1. When Defending:
Pressure and Delay:
It is your responsibility to put pressure (High, Medium, or Low Pressure) on the ball if you are the closest defender to the attacker in CENTRAL AREAS of the field, delay the attacking player from penetrating forward with the ball.
Speed, Angle of approach and Jockeying are key considerations.
Cover and Depth behind the ball:
When the ball is in Central Midfield areas of the field,
Provide cover to your teammate putting pressure on the ball.
When providing cover, communication, angle and distance of support are key considerations.
Balance: Provide cover and balance when ball is in wide areas of field.
Positioning, Discipline and awareness of opponent's positions are key considerations.
Holding role requires Discipline

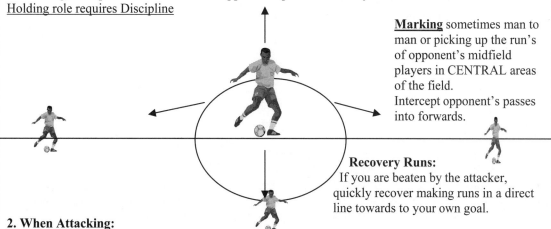

Marking sometimes man to man or picking up the run's of opponent's midfield players in CENTRAL areas of the field.
Intercept opponent's passes into forwards.

Recovery Runs:
If you are beaten by the attacker, quickly recover making runs in a direct line towards to your own goal.

2. When Attacking:
Penetration, When you win the ball, in transition, can you go forward, by either passing, dribbling, VISION.
Provide quality distribution to defenders, midfield players and forwards, short passes, driven passes and long- lofted passes into space in front and behind opponents. Diagonal passes to switch play. If facing your own goal play a supporting pass to defenders - goalkeeper
If in a position in and around opponent's penalty area, can you shoot to score?
Length Depth: Provide depth by identifying and moving into spaces in front of the back 4 defenders.
Intercept opponent's passes into forwards, then look to penetrate.
Mobility: Provide good movement off the ball; however Discipline is required in your role as a holding player within the system. If you get into advanced position, other midfield player needs to balance.

Playing Roles Central Midfield (Attacking)
4 – 4 – 2 Formation

<table>
<tr><td>

Role in Defense:
- Good communication.
- Marking and tracking opponents in central areas of the field.
- **Pressure** on the ball and support your midfield / defenders when play is in central areas of the field.
- **Cover and Balance** when ball on opposite sides of the field.

</td><td>

Role in Attack:
- Good communication.
- Be available to receive a pass, play maker.
- Quality **Distribution** to midfield / forward players.
- **Support** midfield / forwards with good
- **Mobility** movement off the ball

</td></tr>
</table>

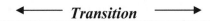 *Transition*

1. When Defending:
Pressure and Delay:

It is your responsibility to put <u>pressure</u> on the ball (High, Medium or Low Pressure) if you are the closest defender to the attacker in CENTRAL AREAS of the field, delay the attacking player from penetrating forward with the ball.

Speed, Angle of approach and Jockeying are key considerations.

Cover and Depth behind the ball:

When the ball is in CENTRAL areas of the field,

Provide <u>cover</u> to your teammate putting pressure on the ball. When providing cover, communication, angle and distance of support are key considerations

Balance: Provide cover and balance when ball is in wide areas of field.

Positioning, Awareness of opponent's positions are ▪ key considerations.

Recovery Runs:

If you are beaten by the attacker

Quickly recover making runs in a direct line towards to your own goal.

Although this player is more attacking minded

The Play maker also has defending responsibilities

Look to delay,

Channel oppositions attack

2. When Attacking:
Penetration,

When you win the ball, in transition,

can you go forward, by either passing, dribbling.

<u>Provide quality distribution</u> to midfield players and forwards, short passes, wall passes, driven passes and long- lofted passes into space in front and behind opponents. Diagonal passes to change point of attack. If in a position in and around opponent's penalty area, can you shoot to score?

Length Depth

Provide length and depth in central areas, look to get into spaces to receive the ball in between opponents midfield and defending units, then look to penetrate.

Mobility

Provide good movement off the ball, Runs in behind opponents defending line, when on the ball run at opponents, through central areas, be creative.

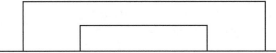

Role in Defense:
- Good communication.
- Marking and tracking opponent on your side of the field.
- **Pressure** on the ball and support your right defender when play is on your side of the field.
- **Cover and Balance** when ball on opposite side of the field.

Role in Attack:
- Good communication.
- Be available to receive a pass. **Width.**
- Distribution to midfield / forward player. **Penetrate**
- **Support** to defenders / midfield / forwards
- **Mobility** good movement off the ball.

← Transition →

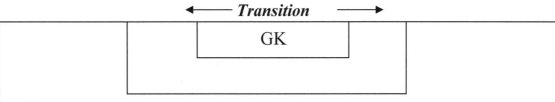

GK

1. When Defending:
Pressure and Delay:
It is your responsibility to put <u>pressure</u> on the ball (high, medium or low pressure) if you are the closest defender to the attacker on <u>the right side</u> of the field, delay the attacking player from penetrating forward with the ball. Speed, Angle of approach and Jockeying are key considerations.

Cover and Depth behind the ball:
When the ball is in your area of the field, Provide <u>cover</u> to your teammate who is putting pressure on the ball. When providing cover, communication, angle and distance of support are key considerations.

Balance:
Provide cover and balance when ball is in <u>wide and opposite areas of field.</u> Positioning, Awareness of opponent's positions are key considerations.

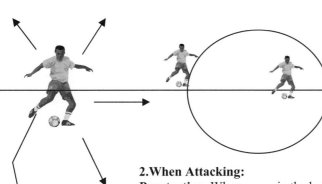

Recovery Runs:
If you are beaten by the attacker Quickly recover, <u>mark and track run's</u> of opponents midfield players.

2. When Attacking:
Penetration, When you win the ball, in transition, can you go forward, by either <u>passing, dribbling or running with the ball.</u>
<u>Provide quality distribution</u> to defender, midfield players and forwards, short passes, wall passes, driven passes. <u>Quality crosses into near, central and far post areas of the box</u>. Long- lofted passes into space in front and behind opponents. Diagonal passes to change point of attack.
If in a position in and around opponent's penalty area, can you <u>shoot to score?</u>
Width Length and Depth
Provide <u>width</u> length and depth by identifying and moving into spaces. Be available to receive a pass
Mobility
Provide good movement off the ball, <u>Diagonal and blind side runs</u> in behind opponents defending line, getting on the end of crosses, when on the ball dribble and take on opponents, be creative.

Playing Roles Left Midfielder
4 – 4 – 2 Formation

Role in Defense:	Role in Attack:
• Good communication. • Marking and tracking opponent on your side of the field. • **Pressure** on the ball and support your right defender when play is on your side of the field. • **Cover and Balance** when ball on opposite side of the field.	• Good communication. • Be available to receive a pass. **Width.** • Distribution to midfield / forward player. **Penetrate** • **Support** to defenders / midfield / forwards • **Mobility** good movement off the ball.

Transitione ← →

GK

1. When Defending:
Pressure and Delay:
It is your responsibility to put <u>pressure</u> on the ball (high, medium or low pressure) if you are the closest defender to the attacker on the <u>left side</u> of the field, delay the attacking player from penetrating forward with the ball. Speed, Angle of approach and Jockeying are key considerations.

Cover and Depth behind the ball:
When the ball is in your area of the field, Provide <u>cover</u> to your teammate who is putting pressure on the ball. When providing cover, communication, angle and distance of support are key considerations.

Balance:
Provide cover and balance when ball is in <u>wide and opposite areas of field.</u>
Positioning, awareness of opponent's
Positions are key considerations.

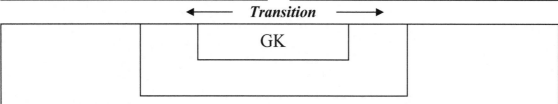

Recovery Runs:
If you are beaten by the attacker
Quickly recover,
<u>mark and track run's</u> of opponents midfield players.

2.When Attacking:
Penetration, When you win the ball, in transition, can you go forward,
by either <u>passing, dribbling or running with the ball.</u>
<u>Provide quality distribution</u> to defender, midfield players and forwards,
short passes, wall passes, driven passes. <u>Quality crosses into near, central and far post areas of the box</u> .
Long- lofted passes into space in front and behind opponents.
Diagonal passes to change point of attack.
If in a position in and around opponent's penalty area, can you <u>shoot to score?</u>

Width Length and Depth
Provide <u>Width</u> Length and depth by identifying and moving into spaces. Be available to receive a pass

Mobility
Provide good movement off the ball, <u>Diagonal and blind side runs</u> in behind opponents defending line, getting on the end of crosses, when on the ball dribble and take on opponents, be creative.

Playing Roles Forwards
In the Midfield 1/3 rd
4 – 4 – 2 Formation

<table>
<tr><td>

Role in Defense:
- Good communication.
- **Pressure** on the ball and support your midfield when play is in central areas of the field. **WIN THE BALL BACK.**
- **Cover and Balance** when ball moves around the field.
  Stay connected Keep shape
  Provide length

</td><td>

Role in Attack:
- Good communication.
- Create opportunity's to score – **Penetrate.** Combination play with midfield / forwards **Support.**
- Good movement off the ball to create your own space and space for others - **Mobility.**
- **<u>Retain possession in midfield 1/3rd</u>**

</td></tr>
</table>

← *Transition* →

1. When Defending:
Pressure and Delay:
It is your responsibility to put pressure on the ball (high, medium or low pressure) if you are the closest defender to the attacker , <u>defend from the front</u> , position yourself and delay the attacking player from penetrating forward with the ball. If you lose possession can you regain it quickly?
Force mistakes from defenders.
Speed, Angle of approach, jockeying and <u>channeling</u> are key considerations.

Cover and Depth behind the ball:
When the ball is in your area of the field,
Provide cover to your teammate who is putting pressure on the ball.
When providing cover,
Communication, angles and distances of support,
are key considerations.

Balance:
At times you may need to recover and fill in for teammate who are caught out of position,

Track opponent's runs.

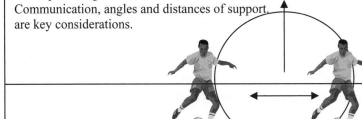

2. When Attacking:
Penetration, When you win the ball, in transition, can you go forward, by either, passing, dribbling or running with the ball.
<u>Provide quality distribution</u> to link up with midfield players and other forward, short passes, wall passes, driven passes, long- lofted passes into space behind opponents.
Diagonal passes to change point of attack.
Length and Depth
Provide length and depth by identifying and moving into spaces. Be always available to receive a pass, look to retain possession in midfield 1/3rd by controlling and shielding, then look to link up with supporting fullbacks and midfield players
Create and Exploit the space behind and in front at every opportunity either with or without the ball.
Mobility
Provide good movement by <u>checking away</u> from defenders towards the ball in midfield areas.
Recognize fellow striker's movement and move intelligently off them.

Playing Roles Forwards / 2 strikers
In and around the Box (Final 1/3)
4 – 4 – 2 Formation

Role in Defense:	Role in Attack:

• Good communication.
• **Pressure** on the ball.
• Force the play sideways and backwards when possible.
• **Cover and Balance** when ball moves around the field.
  Stay compact - Keep shape.
	• Good communication.
	• **Penetrate "SHOOT"**
	  Create opportunity's to score.
	• **Support** Combination play with midfield / forwards
	• **Mobility** Good movement off the ball to create your own space and space for others.
	• <u>**Retain Possession in Final 1/3rd**</u>

← *Transition* →

1. When Defending:

Pressure:

It is your responsibility to put pressure on the ball. Force mistakes from defenders, don't allow defenders to get out of there own defensive 1/3rd.

Pressure individually / collectively, feed off defender's mistakes.

Cover and Depth behind the ball:

Provide cover to your teammate who is putting pressure on the ball.

When providing cover, communication, angles distances of support.

<u>Channeling</u> are key considerations.

Balance:

At times may need to recover and fill in for team-mate who are caught out of position.

2. When Attacking:

Penetration, After receiving the ball, can you go forward, by either, passing, combination play, wall passes, Take over's, 1 and 2 touch speed of play , dribbling, running at defenders looking to create scoring opportunities. Shoot at any opportunity, be creative take risks.

Express your skill and imagination.

Length and Depth

Provide length and depth by identifying and moving into spaces.

Create and Exploit the space behind and in front at every opportunity either with the ball or without the ball.

Mobility (Speed and pace)

Intelligent movement across the line of defenders on the edge of the box. Diagonal runs in front and behind defenders creating space for self and others. Recognize fellow striker's movement and move intelligently off them. In and around the box near and far post runs to attack crosses from wide areas.

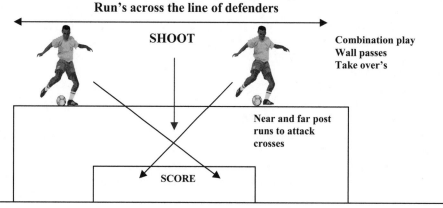

Variation's on player organization
4 – 4 – 2 Formation
Flat Back 4 / Diamond Midfield 4

Goalkeeper	Defending Unit Flat Back 4	Midfield Unit Diamond 4	2 Strikers
1	1 Right defender 2 Central defenders 1 Left defender	1 Right Midfield 1 Central Midfield (Holding) 1 Central Midfield (Attacking) 1 Left Midfield	1 left 1 right

TEAM SHAPE WHEN DEFENDING ←→ **TEAM SHAPE WHEN ATTACKING**

TRANSITION

Compact position in relation to where the ball moves   Provide length width, and depth to create space

Variation's on player organization
4 – 4 – 2 Formation
Flat Back 4 / Flat Midfield 4

Goalkeeper	Defending Unit Flat Back 4	Midfield Unit Flat 4	2 Strikers
1	1 Right defender 2 Central defenders 1 Left defender	1 Outside Right Midfield 1 Inside Right midfield 1 Inside Left midfield 1 Outside Left Midfield	1 left 1 right

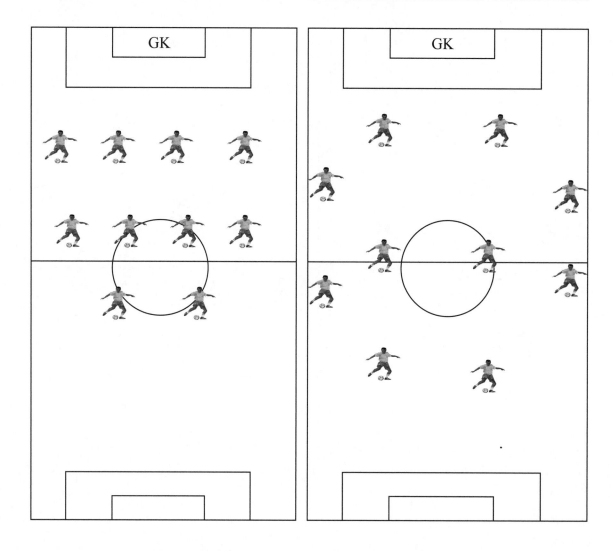

TEAM SHAPE WHEN DEFENDING ⟷ **TEAM SHAPE WHEN ATTACKING**

TRANSITION

Compact position in relation to where the ball moves   Provide length width, and depth to create space

Variation's on player organization
4 – 4 – 2 Formation
Diamond Back 4 / Flat Midfield 4

Goalkeeper	Defending Unit Diamond Back 4	Midfield Unit Flat 4	2 Strikers
1	1 Right defender 1 Central defenders Sweeper 1 Central Defender Stopper 1 Left defender	1 Outside Right Midfield 1 Inside Right midfield 1 Inside Left midfield 1 Outside Left Midfield	1 left 1 right

TEAM SHAPE WHEN DEFENDING   **TEAM SHAPE WHEN ATTACKING**

←——————→

TRANSITION

Compact position in relation to where the ball moves   Provide length width, and depth to create space

Chapter 5
Player's role and responsibilities
In a 4-3-3 system of play

- **Goalkeeper role in a 4-3-3**

Refer to 4-4-2 presentation on page 22

- **Right Defender role in a 4-3-3**

Refer to 4-4-2 presentation on page 23

- **Left Defender role in a 4-3-3**

Refer to 4-4-2 presentation on page 24

- **Central Defender Right**

Refer to 4-4-2 presentation on page 25

- **Central Defender Left**

Refer to 4-4-2 presentation on page 26

The back 4 defending player's roles and responsibilities are the same in a 4-3-3 and 4-4-2 system of play

Playing Roles Central Midfield (Holding)
4 – 3 – 3 Formation

<table>
<tr>
<td>

Role in Defense:
- Good communication.
- Marking and tracking opponents in central areas of the field.
- **Pressure** on the ball and support your midfield / defenders. when play is in central areas of the field.
- **Cover and Balance** when ball on opposite sides of the field.

</td>
<td>

Role in Attack:
- Good communication.
- Be available to receive a pass.
- Quality **Distribution** to defenders / midfield / forward players.
- **Support** to defenders / midfield / forwards with good movement off the ball - **Mobility**

</td>
</tr>
</table>

← *Transition* →

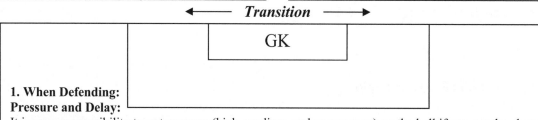

GK

1. When Defending:
Pressure and Delay:
It is your responsibility to put <u>pressure</u> (high, medium, or low pressure) on the ball if you are the closest defender to the attacker in <u>CENTRAL AREAS of the field</u>, delay the attacking player from penetrating forward with the ball.
Speed, Angle of approach and Jockeying are key considerations.
Cover and Depth behind the ball:
When the ball is in <u>Central Midfield</u> areas of the field,
Provide <u>cover</u> to your teammate putting pressure on the ball.
When providing cover, communication, angle and distance of support, <u>staying compact are key considerations, when playing with 3 in the midfield 1/3rd</u>.
Balance: Provide cover and balance when ball is in wide areas of field.
Positioning, Discipline and awareness of opponent's positions are key considerations.
<u>Holding role requires Discipline</u>

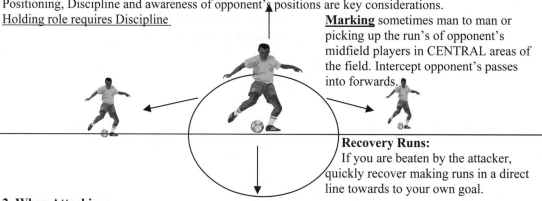

Marking sometimes man to man or picking up the run's of opponent's midfield players in CENTRAL areas of the field. Intercept opponent's passes into forwards.

Recovery Runs:
If you are beaten by the attacker, quickly recover making runs in a direct line towards to your own goal.

2. When Attacking:
Penetration, When you win the ball, in transition, can you go forward, by either passing, dribbling, <u>VISION.</u>
<u>Provide quality distribution</u> to defenders, midfield players and forwards, short passes, driven passes and long- lofted passes into space in front and behind opponents. Diagonal passes to switch play. If facing your own goal play a supporting pass to defenders - goalkeeper
If in a position in and around opponent's penalty area, can you shoot to score?
Length Depth: Provide depth by identifying and moving into spaces in front of the back 4 defenders.
<u>Intercept opponent's passes into forwards, then look to penetrate.</u>
Mobility: Provide good movement off the ball; however <u>Discipline is required</u> in your role as a holding player within the system. If you get into advanced position, other midfield player needs to balance.

Playing Roles In-side Right Midfielder
4 – 3 – 3 System

<table>
<tr><td>

Role in Defense:
- Good communication.
- Marking and tracking opponent on your side of the field.
- **Pressure** on the ball and support your right defender when play is on your side of the field.
- **Cover and Balance** when ball on opposite side of the field.

</td><td>

Role in Attack:
- Good communication.
- Be available to receive a pass. **Width.**
- Distribution to midfield / forward player. **Penetrate**
- **Support** to defenders / midfield, forwards.
- **Mobility -** good movement off the ball

</td></tr>
</table>

← *Transition* →

GK

1. When Defending:
Pressure and Delay:
It is your responsibility to put <u>pressure</u> on the ball (high, medium or low pressure) if you are the closest defender to the attacker <u>on the right side </u>of the field, delay the attacking player from penetrating forward with the ball.
Speed, Angle of approach and Jockeying are key considerations.
Cover and Depth behind the ball:
When the ball is in your area of the field, Provide <u>cover</u> to your teammate who is putting pressure on the ball.

When providing cover, communication, angle and distance of support, <u>staying compact are key considerations, when playing with 3 in the midfield 1/3rd</u> .

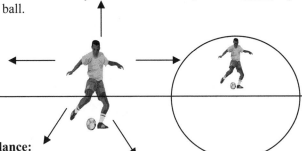

Balance:
Provide cover and balance when ball is in wide and opposite areas of field.
Positioning, Awareness of opponent's positions are key considerations.
Recovery Runs:
 If you are beaten by the attacker, quickly recover, mark and track run's of opponents midfield players.
2. When Attacking:
Penetration, When you win the ball, in transition, can you go forward, by either Passing, Dribbling.
Provide quality distribution to midfield players and forwards, short passes, wall passes, driven passes, crosses into the box and long- lofted passes into space in front and behind opponents.
Diagonal passes to change point of attack.
If in a position in and around opponent's penalty area, can you shoot to score?
Width and Depth
Provide width and depth by identifying and moving into spaces. Be available to receive a pass
Mobility
Provide good movement off the ball, to support back 4 , forward runs from deep positions in behind opponents defending line, getting on the end of crosses, when on the ball dribble and take on opponents in attacking areas, be creative.

Playing Roles In-side Left Midfielder
4 – 3 – 3 System

<table>
<tr><td>

Role in Defense:
- Good communication.
- Marking and tracking opponent on your side of the field.
- **Pressure** on the ball and support your right defender when play is on your side of the field.
- **Cover and Balance** when ball on opposite side of the field.

</td><td>

Role in Attack:
- Good communication.
- Be available to receive a pass. **Width.**
- Distribution to midfield / forward player. **Penetrate**
- **Support** to Defenders / midfield / forwards.
- **Mobility -** good movement off the ball

</td></tr>
</table>

← *Transition* →

GK

1. When Defending:

Pressure and Delay:

It is your responsibility to put <u>pressure</u> on the ball (high, medium or low pressure) if you are the closest defender to the attacker <u>on the left side</u> of the field, delay the attacking player from penetrating forward with the ball.

Speed, Angle of approach and Jockeying are key considerations.

Cover and Depth behind the ball:

When the ball is in your area of the field, Provide <u>cover</u> to your teammate who is putting pressure on the ball. When providing cover, communication, angle and distance of support, <u>staying compact are key considerations,</u> when playing with 3 in the midfield 1/3rd.

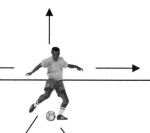

Balance:

Provide cover and balance

When ball is in wide and opposite areas of field.

Positioning, Awareness of opponent's positions are key considerations.

Recovery Runs:

If you are beaten by the attacker, quickly recover, mark and track run's of opponents midfield players.

2. When Attacking:

Penetration, When you win the ball, in transition, can you go forward, by either Passing, Dribbling. Provide quality distribution to midfield players and forwards, short passes, wall passes, driven passes, crosses into the box and long- lofted passes into space in front and behind opponents.

Diagonal passes to change point of attack.

When on the ball dribble and take on opponents in attacking areas, be creative.

If in a position in and around opponent's penalty area, can you shoot to score?

Width and Depth

Provide width and depth by identifying and moving into spaces. Be available to receive a pass

Mobility

Provide good movement off the ball, to support back 4 , forward runs from deep positions in behind opponents defending line, getting on the end of crosses.

42

<table>
<tr><td>

Role in Defense:

- Good communication.
- **Pressure** on the ball and support your midfield when play is in central areas of the field. **WIN THE BALL BACK.**
- **Cover and Balance** when ball moves around the field.
  Stay connected - Keep shape
  Provide length

</td><td>

Role in Attack:

- Good communication.
- Create opportunity's to score – **Penetrate.** Combination plays midfield, forwards
- **Support,** Good movement off the ball to create your own space and space for others **Mobility.**
- <u>**Retain possession in midfield 1/3rd**</u>

</td></tr>
</table>

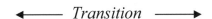

← *Transition* →

1. When Defending:
Pressure and Delay:
It is your responsibility to put pressure on the ball (high, medium or low pressure) if you are the closest defender to the attacker <u>in Right flank area's</u> , defend from the front , position yourself and delay the attacking player from penetrating forward with the ball. If you lose possession can you regain it quickly? Force mistakes from defenders, midfield players
Speed, Angle of approach, Jockeying and channeling are key considerations.
Cover and Depth behind the ball:
When the ball is in your area of the field,
Provide cover to your teammate who is putting pressure on the ball.

When providing cover, communication, angles and distances of support, are key considerations.
Balance: At times may need to recover and fill in for teammate who are caught out of position, Track opponent's runs and provide cover for midfield and fullbacks when needed

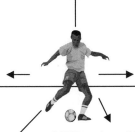

2.When Attacking:
Penetration, When you win the ball, in transition, can you go forward, by either, passing, dribbling, or running with the ball into spaces behind the opponent's defense? Provide quality distribution to link up with midfield players, forwards and fullback, short passes, wall passes, driven passes, Long- lofted passes into space behind opponents.
Diagonal passes to change point of attack.
Width Length and Depth,
<u>Provide Width</u> length and depth by identifying and moving into spaces.
 Be always available to receive a pass; look to retain possession in midfield 1/3rd by controlling and shielding with back to goal, then link up with supporting midfield , fullback and forward players.
Create and Exploit the space behind and in front at every opportunity either with the ball or without the ball
Mobility, Provide good movement by checking away from defender towards the ball <u>in wide midfield areas</u>, Recognize fellow striker's movement and move intelligently off them. <u>Interchange positions with</u> other strikers.

Playing Roles Central Forward
In the Midfield 1/3 ʳᵈ
4 – 3 – 3 System

<table>
<tr>
<td>

Role in Defense:
- Good communication.
- **Pressure** on the ball and support your midfield when play is in central areas of the field. **WIN THE BALL BACK.**
- **Cover and Balance** when ball moves around the field. Stay connected Keep shape – Provide length

</td>
<td>

Role in Attack:
- Good communication.
- Create opportunity's to score – **Penetrate.**
- Combination plays with midfield / forwards **Support.**
- Good movement off the ball to create your own space and space for others - **Mobility.**
- <u>**Retain possession in midfield 1/3ʳᵈ**</u>

</td>
</tr>
</table>

← *Transition* →

1. When Defending:

Pressure and Delay: It is your responsibility to put pressure on the ball (high, medium or low pressure) if you are the closest defender to the attacker in <u>central areas</u> , defend from the front , position yourself and delay the attacking player from penetrating forward with the ball. If you lose possession can you regain it quickly? Force mistakes from defenders, midfield players, Speed, Angle of approach, Jockeying and channeling are key considerations.

Cover and Depth behind the ball: When the ball is in central areas of the field,
Provide cover to your teammate who is putting pressure on the ball.
When providing cover, Communication, angles and distances of support are key considerations.

Balance:
At times may need to recover and fill in for teammate who are caught out of position, Track opponent's runs and provide cover for <u>midfield players</u> when needed

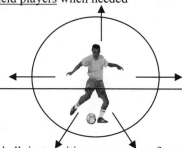

2. When Attacking:

Penetration, When you win the ball, in transition, can you go forward, by either, passing, dribbling, or running with the ball into spaces behind the opponent's defense?
Provide quality distribution to link up with midfield players and forwards and fullback, short passes, wall passes, driven passes, Diagonal passes to change point of attack into spaces behind opponent's defense.

Length and Depth
<u>Provide length and depth</u> by identifying and moving into spaces. Be always available to receive a pass; look to retain possession in midfield 1/3ʳᵈ by <u>controlling and shielding with your back to goal</u>, then link up with supporting midfield, fullback and other forward players.
Create and Exploit the space behind and in front at every opportunity either with the ball or without the ball
Mobility Provide good movement by checking away from defender towards the ball in midfield areas. Recognize fellow striker's movements and move intelligently off them. <u>Interchange positions with</u> other strikers.

Playing Roles Left Forward
In the Midfield 1/3 rd
4 – 3 – 3 System

<table>
<tr>
<td>

Role in Defense:
- Good communication.
- **Pressure** on the ball and support your midfield when play is in central areas of the field. **WIN THE BALL BACK.**
- **Cover and Balance** when ball moves around the field.
   Stay connected - Keep shape
   Provide length

</td>
<td>

Role in Attack:
- Good communication.
- Create opportunity's to score – **Penetrate.** Combination plays midfield, forwards
- **Support,** Good movement off the ball to create your own space and space for others **Mobility.**
- <u>**Retain possession in midfield 1/3rd**</u>

</td>
</tr>
</table>

◄——— *Transition* ———►

1. When Defending:
Pressure and Delay:
It is your responsibility to put pressure on the ball (high, medium or low pressure) if you are the closest defender to the attacker <u>in left flank area's</u> , defend from the front , position yourself and delay the attacking player from penetrating forward with the ball. If you lose possession can you regain it quickly? Force mistakes from defenders, midfield players
Speed, Angle of approach, Jockeying and channeling are key considerations.
Cover and Depth behind the ball:
When the ball is in left flank areas of the field,
Provide cover to your teammate who is putting pressure on the ball.

When providing cover, communication, angles and distances of support, are key considerations.
Balance:
At times may need to recover and fill in for teammate who are caught out of position,
Track opponent's runs and provide cover for midfield and fullbacks when needed

 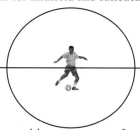 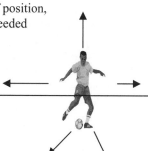

2.When Attacking:
Penetration, When you win the ball, in transition, can you go forward, by either
passing, dribbling, or running with the ball into spaces behind the opponent's defense?
 Provide quality distribution to link up with midfield players and forwards and fullback,
Short passes, wall passes, driven passes also long- lofted passes into space behind opponents.
 Diagonal passes to change point of attack.

Width Length and Depth, <u>Provide Width</u> length and depth by identifying and moving into spaces.
 Be always available to receive a pass; look to retain possession in midfield 1/3rd by controlling and shielding with back to goal, then link up with supporting midfield , fullback and forward players.
Create and Exploit the space behind and in front at every opportunity either with the ball or without the ball
Mobility, Provide good movement by checking away from defender towards the ball <u>in wide midfield areas</u>, Recognize fellow striker's movement and move intelligently off them. <u>Interchange positions with other strikers.</u>

Playing Roles Right Forward
In Attacking 1/3
4 – 3 – 3 System

<table>
<tr><td>

Role in Defense:
- Good communication.
- **Pressure** on the ball.
- Force the play sideways and backwards when possible.
- **Cover and Balance** when ball moves around the field.
   Stay connected - Keep shape.

</td><td>

Role in Attack:
- Good communication.
- **SHOOT** / Create opportunity's to score - **Penetrate**
- Combination play with midfield / forwards - **Support**
- Good movement off the ball to create your own space and space for others – **Mobility**
- <u>**Retain Possession in Final 1/3rd**</u>

</td></tr>
</table>

 ← *Transition* →

1. When Defending:

Pressure: It is your responsibility to put pressure on the ball. Force mistakes from defenders, don't allow defenders to get out of there own defensive 1/3rd. Pressure individually / collectively,
Feed of those mistakes.

Cover and Depth behind the ball: Provide cover to your teammate who is putting pressure on the ball. When providing cover, communication, angles distances of support.
Channeling are key considerations.

Balance: At times may need to recover and fill in for teammate who are caught out of position,
 Track opponent's run

2.When Attacking:

Penetration, After receiving the ball, can you go forward, by either, passing combination play, wall passes, Take over's, 1 and 2 touch speed of play , dribbling, running at defenders 1 v1 looking to get quality crosses into the penalty area to create scoring opportunities,
 Shoot at any opportunity, be creative take risks, express your skill and imagination.

Width Length and Depth

<u>Provide Width length and depth</u> by identifying and moving into spaces. Create and Exploit the space behind and in front at every opportunity either with the ball or without the ball .

Mobility (Speed and pace)

Intelligent movement across the line of defenders on the edge of the box. Diagonal runs in front and behind defenders creating space for self and others. Recognize fellow striker's movement and move intelligently off them. In and around the box near and far post runs to attack crosses from wide areas.

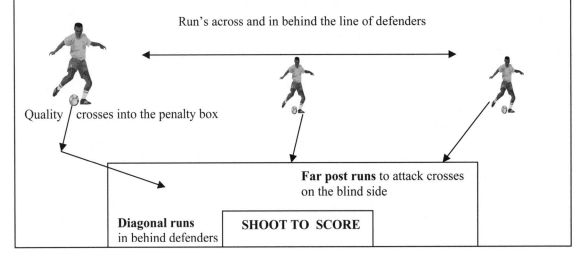

Run's across and in behind the line of defenders

Quality crosses into the penalty box

Far post runs to attack crosses on the blind side

Diagonal runs in behind defenders

SHOOT TO SCORE

Role in Defense:	Role in Attack:
• Good communication. • **Pressure** on the ball. • Force the play sideways and backwards when possible. • **Cover and Balance** when ball moves around the field. Stay connected - Keep shape.	• Good communication. • **SHOOT** / Create opportunity's to score - **Penetrate** • Combination play with midfield / forwards - **Support** • Good movement off the ball to create your own space and space for others – **Mobility** • <u>**Retain Possession in Final 1/3rd**</u>

Transition

1. When Defending:

Pressure: It is your responsibility to put pressure on the ball. Force mistakes from defenders, don't allow defenders to get out of there own defensive 1/3rd . Pressure individually / collectively , Feed of those mistakes.

Cover and Depth behind the ball: Provide cover to your teammate who is putting pressure on the ball. When providing cover, communication,angles distances of support.
Channeling are key considerations.

Balance: At times may need to recover and fill in for teammate who are caught out of position, Track opponent's runs out of the back

2.When Attacking:

Penetration, After receiving the ball, can you go forward, by either, passing combination play, wall passes, Take over's, 1 and 2 touch speed of play , dribbling, running at defenders 1 v1 looking to get into the <u>penalty area</u> to create scoring opportunities, Shoot at any opportunity.
Be creative take risks express your skill and imagination.

Length and Depth
<u>Provide length and depth</u> by identifying and moving into spaces. Create and Exploit the space behind and in front at every opportunity either with the ball or without the ball.

Mobility (Speed and pace)
Intelligent movement across the line of defenders on the edge of the box. Diagonal runs in front and behind defenders creating space for self and others. Recognize fellow striker's movement and move intelligently off them. <u>In and around the box near and far post runs to attack crosses from wide areas.</u>

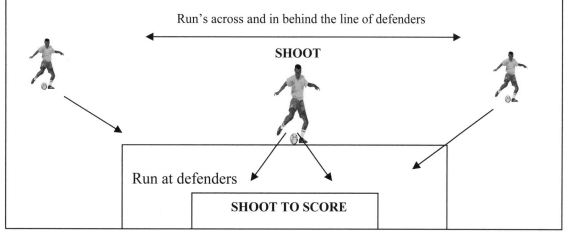

Run's across and in behind the line of defenders

SHOOT

Run at defenders

SHOOT TO SCORE

Playing Roles Left Forward
In Attacking 1/3
4 – 3 – 3 System

Role in Defense:	Role in Attack:
• Good communication.	• Good communication.
• **Pressure** on the ball.	• **SHOOT** / Create opportunity's to score - **Penetrate**
• Force the play sideways and backwards when possible.	• Combination play with midfield / forwards - **Support**
• **Cover and Balance** when ball moves around the field. Stay connected - Keep shape.	• Good movement off the ball to create your own space and space for others – **Mobility**
	• <u>**Retain Possession in Final 1/3rd**</u>

◄ ── *Transition* ──►

1. When Defending:

Pressure: It is your responsibility to put pressure on the ball. Force mistakes from defenders, don't allow defenders to get out of there own defensive 1/3rd . Pressure individually / collectively,
Feed of those mistakes.

Cover and Depth behind the ball: Provide cover to your teammate who is putting pressure on the ball. When providing cover, communication, angles distances of support.
Channeling are key considerations.

Balance: At times may need to recover and fill in for teammate who are caught out of position,
 Track opponent's run

2.When Attacking:

Penetration, After receiving the ball, can you go forward, by either, passing combination play, wall passes, Take over's, 1 and 2 touch speed of play , dribbling, running at defenders 1 v1 looking to get quality crosses into the penalty area to create scoring opportunities,
 Shoot at any opportunity, Be creative take risks, express your skill and imagination.

Width Length and Depth

<u>Provide Width length and depth</u> by identifying and moving into spaces. Create and Exploit the space behind and in front at every opportunity either with the ball or without the ball .

Mobility (Speed and pace)

Intelligent movement across the line of defenders on the edge of the box. Diagonal runs in front and behind defenders creating space for self and others. Recognize fellow striker's movement and move intelligently off them. In and around the box near and far post runs to attack crosses from wide areas.

Run's across and in behind the line of defenders

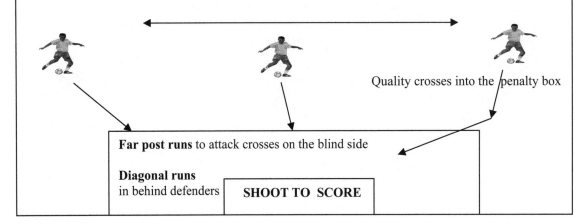

Quality crosses into the penalty box

Far post runs to attack crosses on the blind side

Diagonal runs
in behind defenders   **SHOOT TO SCORE**

Variation's on player organization
4 – 3 – 3 Formation
Flat Back 4 / Flat Midfield 3

Goalkeeper	Defending Unit Flat Back 4	Midfield Unit Flat 3	3 Strikers
1	1 Right defender 2 Central defenders 1 Left defender	1 Right Midfield 1 Central Midfield (Holding) 1 Left Midfield	1 left 1 Central 1 right

TEAM SHAPE WHEN DEFENDING   **TEAM SHAPE WHEN ATTACKING**

← **TRANSITION** →

Compact position in relation to where the ball moves   Provide length width, and depth to create space

Variation's on player organization
4 – 3 – 3 Formation
Flat Back 4 / Triangle Midfield 3

Goalkeeper	Defending Unit Flat Back 4	Midfield Unit Triangle 3	3 Strikers
1	1 Right defender 2 Central defenders 1 Left defender	1 Inside Right midfield 1 Inside Left midfield 1 Central holding midfield	1 left 1 right 1 Central

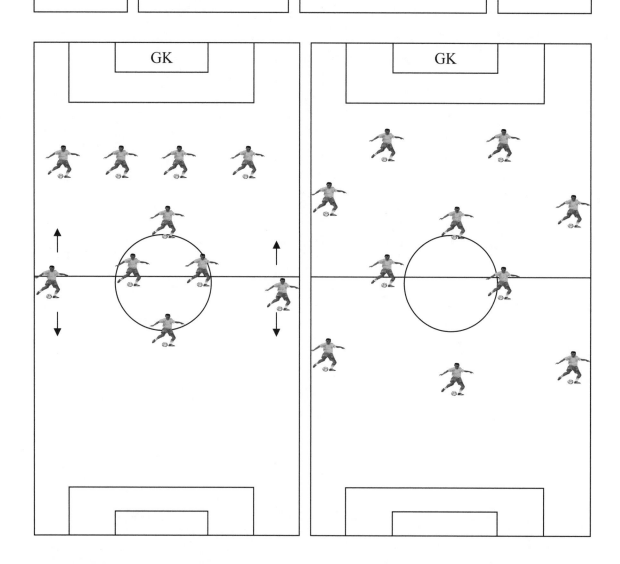

TEAM SHAPE WHEN DEFENDING   **TEAM SHAPE WHEN ATTACKING**

TRANSITION

Compact position in relation to where the ball moves   Provide length width, and depth to create space
2 outside players recover to provide cover on flanks

Chapter 6
Player's role and responsibilities
In a 3-5-2 system of play

Playing Roles Central Defender (Left Side)
3 – 5 – 2 Formation

Role in Defense:	Role in Attack:
• Good communication. • Mark attackers as directed,zonal,man to man • **Pressure** and support when play is central areas of the field. • **Cover and Balance** when ball is on wide areas of the field.	• Good communication. • Be available to receive a pass , **Width / Depth** • Quality **Distribution** to midfield / forward players. • Provide **Support** to defenders / midfield / forwards.

←———— *Transition* ————→

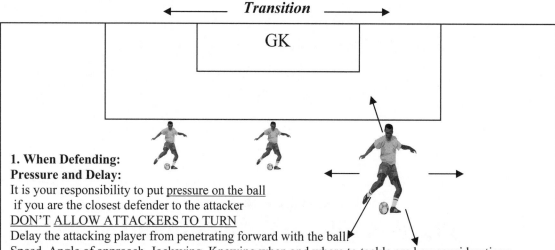

GK

1. When Defending:
Pressure and Delay:
It is your responsibility to put <u>pressure on the ball</u>
 if you are the closest defender to the attacker
<u>DON'T ALLOW ATTACKERS TO TURN</u>
Delay the attacking player from penetrating forward with the ball
Speed, Angle of approach, Jockeying, Knowing <u>when and where</u> to tackle are key considerations,
<u>When selecting and playing 3 at the back players need to be strong and good 1 v 1 defenders.</u>
Cover and Depth behind the ball:
When the ball is on your side of the field, provide cover to your teammate who is putting pressure on the ball. When providing cover, communication, angle and distance of support are key considerations.
<u>Cover in the flank areas is needed and should be provided by your outside midfield players</u>
Balance:
Provide cover and balance when ball is in wide areas of field.
Positioning either zonal / man to man, awareness of opponent's positions are key considerations.
Mark , and track runs of attackers in <u>left central</u> areas of the field. Passing marking responsibilities on to other defenders is also a key consideration when opponents move across the defending line.
Good communication between the back 3 is needed when doing so.
Keep Shape <u>– Stay Compact on the left side of centre in your group of 3</u> ,
Form partnership with other central defender, and outside midfield player.
Recovery Runs:
If you are beaten by the attacker, quickly recover making runs in a direct line towards to your own goal.
2.When Attacking:
Penetration: When you win the ball, in transition, can you go forward, by either <u>passing</u>, or <u>running</u> the ball out of defense?
<u>Provide quality distribution</u> to midfield players and forwards, <u>short passes</u>, <u>driven passes</u> and <u>long-lofted passes</u> to start the attack. <u>Also support passes to goalkeeper</u>
Depth: Provide depth by identifying and moving into spaces off the ball, distance and angle of support behind the player with the ball are key considerations, be available at all times to receive a pass.
Mobility: <u>Provide good movement off the ball in a supporting role.</u>

Playing Roles Central Defender
3 – 5 – 2 Formation

<table>
<tr><td>

Role in Defense:
- Good communication.
- Mark attackers as directed,zonal,man to man
- **Pressure** and support when play is central areas of the field.
- **Cover and Balance** when ball is on wide areas of the field.

</td><td>

Role in Attack:
- Good communication.
- Be available to receive a pass , **Width / Depth**
- Quality **Distribution** to midfield / forward players.
- Provide **Support** to defenders / midfield / forwards.

</td></tr>
</table>

Transition ←――――――→

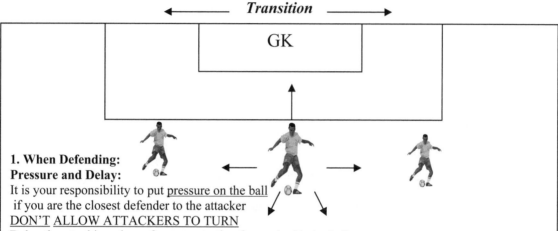

GK

1. When Defending:
Pressure and Delay:
It is your responsibility to put <u>pressure on the ball</u>
if you are the closest defender to the attacker
<u>DON'T</u> <u>ALLOW ATTACKERS TO TURN</u>
Delay the attacking player from penetrating forward with the ball.
Speed, Angle of approach, Jockeying, Knowing <u>when and where</u> to tackle are key considerations,
<u>When selecting and playing 3 at the back players need to be strong and good 1 v 1 defenders.</u>
Cover and Depth behind the ball:
When the ball is on your side of the field, provide cover to your teammate who is putting pressure on the ball. When providing cover, communication, angle and distance of support are key considerations.
Balance:
Provide cover and balance when ball is in wide areas of field.
Positioning either zonal / man to man, awareness of opponent's positions are key considerations.
Mark , and track runs of attackers in <u>central</u> areas of the field. Passing marking responsibilities on to other defenders is also a key consideration when opponents move across the defending line.
Good communication between the back 3 is needed when doing so.
Keep Shape <u>– Stay</u> <u>Compact Centrally in your group of 3</u> ,
Form partnership with other central defender, and outside midfield player.
Recovery Runs:
If you are beaten by the attacker, quickly recover making runs in a direct line towards to your own goal.
2.When Attacking:
Penetration: When you win the ball, in transition, can you go forward, by either <u>passing</u>, or <u>running</u> the ball out of defense?
<u>Provide quality distribution</u> to midfield players and forwards, <u>short passes</u>, <u>driven passes</u> and <u>long-lofted passes</u> to start the attack. <u>Also support passes to goalkeeper</u>
Depth: Provide depth by identifying and moving into spaces off the ball, distance and angle of support behind the player with the ball are key considerations, be available at all times to receive a pass.
Mobility: <u>Provide good movement off the ball in a supporting role.</u>

Playing Roles Right Central Defender
3 – 5 – 2 Formation

Role in Defense:	Role in Attack:
• Good communication. • Mark attackers as directed,zonal,man to man • **Pressure** and support when play is central areas of the field. • **Cover and Balance** when ball is on wide areas of the field.	• Good communication. • Be available to receive a pass , **Width / Depth** • Quality **Distribution** to midfield / forward players. • Provide **Support** to defenders / midfield / forwards.

Transition ←——————→

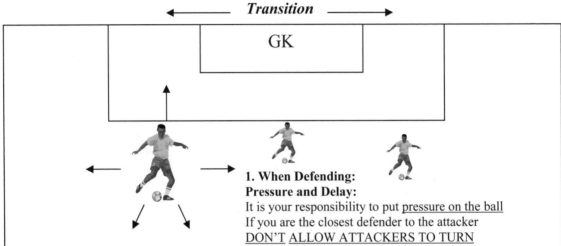

GK

1. When Defending:
Pressure and Delay:
It is your responsibility to put <u>pressure on the ball</u>
If you are the closest defender to the attacker
<u>DON'T ALLOW ATTACKERS TO TURN</u>
Delay the attacking player from penetrating forward with the ball.
Speed, Angle of approach, Jockeying, Knowing <u>when and where</u> to tackle are key considerations,
<u>When selecting and playing 3 at the back players need to be strong and good 1 v 1 defenders.</u>
Cover and Depth behind the ball:
When the ball is on your side of the field, provide cover to your teammate who is putting pressure on the ball. When providing cover, communication, angle and distance of support are key considerations.
Balance:
Provide cover and balance when ball is in wide areas of field.
Positioning either zonal / man to man, awareness of opponent's positions are key considerations.
Mark , and track runs of attackers in <u>Right Central areas</u> of the field. Passing marking responsibilities on to other defenders is also a key consideration when opponents move across the defending line.
Good communication between the back 3 is needed when doing so.
Keep Shape <u>– Stay Compact on the right side of centre in your group of 3</u> ,
Form partnership with other central defender, and outside midfield player.
Recovery Runs:
If you are beaten by the attacker, quickly recover making runs in a direct line towards to your own goal.
2.When Attacking:
Penetration: When you win the ball, in transition, can you go forward, by either <u>passing</u>, or <u>running</u> the ball out of defense?
<u>Provide quality distribution</u> to midfield players and forwards, <u>short passes</u>, <u>driven passes</u> and <u>long-lofted passes</u> to start the attack. <u>Also support passes to goalkeeper</u>
Depth: Provide depth by identifying and moving into spaces off the ball, distance and angle of support behind the player with the ball are key considerations, be available at all times to receive a pass.
Mobility: <u>Provide good movement off the ball in a supporting role.</u>

Playing Roles Right Outside / Winger
3 – 5 – 2 System

<table>
<tr><td>

Role in Defense:
- Good communication.
- **Pressure** on the ball and support your midfield when play is in central areas of the field. **WIN THE BALL BACK.**
- **Cover and Balance** when ball moves around the field.
  Stay connected - Keep shape
  Provide length

</td><td>

Role in Attack:
- Good communication.
- Create opportunity's to score – **Penetrate.** Combination plays midfield, forwards
- **Support,** Good movement off the ball to create your own space and space for others **Mobility.**
- <u>**Retain possession in midfield 1/3rd**</u>

</td></tr>
</table>

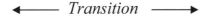

← *Transition* →

1. When Defending:
Pressure and Delay:
It is your responsibility to put pressure on the ball (high, medium or low pressure) if you are the closest defender to the attacker <u>in flank area's</u> , position yourself and delay the attacking player from penetrating forward with the ball. Force mistakes from defenders, midfield players
Speed, Angle of approach, Jockeying and channeling are key considerations.
Cover and Depth behind the ball:
When defending, when the ball is in flank areas <u>it is important to get back and provide cover for your right central</u> <u>defender.</u> When providing cover, communication, angles and distances of support, are key considerations.

Balance: At times may need to recover and fill in for teammate who are caught out of position, Track opponent's runs and provide cover for midfield and right central defenders when needed

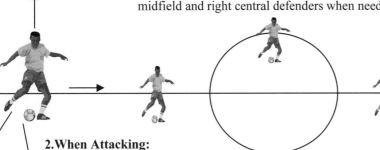

2.When Attacking:
Penetration, When you win the ball, in transition, can you go forward, by either, passing, dribbling, or running with the ball into spaces behind the opponent's defense? Provide quality distribution to link up with midfield players and forwards, short passes, wall passes, driven passes, Long- lofted passes into space behind opponents. Provide quality crosses into the penalty area, as well as diagonal passes to change point of attack.

Width Length and Depth, <u>Provide width</u> length and depth by identifying and moving into spaces.
 Be always available to receive a pass; look to retain possession in midfield 1/3rd by controlling and shielding with back to goal, then link up with supporting midfield and forward players.
Create space by positioning and staying wide at every opportunity being available to receive the ball.
<u>Look to take defenders on 1v 1with speed and pace, creating opportunities to deliver crosses into the</u> <u>penalty area , Time your runs and get on the end of crosses from the opposite side</u>

Mobility, Provide good movement by checking away from opponents towards the ball <u>in wide midfield</u> <u>areas</u>, recognize and time diagonal runs in behind the defending line to exploit the space in behind

Playing Roles Left Outside Winger
3 – 5 – 2 System

<table>
<tr><td>

Role in Defense:
- Good communication.
- **Pressure** on the ball and support your midfield when play is in central areas of the field. **WIN THE BALL BACK.**
- **Cover and Balance** when ball moves around the field.
  Stay connected - Keep shape
  Provide length

</td><td>

Role in Attack:
- Good communication.
- Create opportunity's to score – **Penetrate.** Combination plays midfield, forwards
- **Support,** Good movement off the ball to create your own space and space for others **Mobility.**
- **Retain possession in midfield 1/3rd**

</td></tr>
</table>

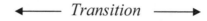 *Transition*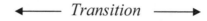

---

1. When Defending:
Pressure and Delay:

It is your responsibility to put pressure on the ball (high, medium or low pressure) if you are the closest defender to the attacker in flank area's , position yourself and delay the attacking player from penetrating forward with the ball. Force mistakes from defenders, midfield players
Speed, Angle of approach, Jockeying and channeling are key considerations.

Cover and Depth behind the ball:

When defending, when the ball is in flank areas it is important to get back and provide cover for your Left central defender. When providing cover, communication, angles and distances of support, are key considerations.

Balance: At times may need to recover and fill in for teammate who are caught out of position, Track opponent's runs and provide cover for midfield and right central defenders when needed

  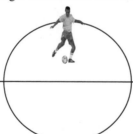 

2.When Attacking:
Penetration, When you win the ball, in transition, can you go forward, by either, passing, dribbling, or running with the ball into spaces behind the opponent's defense? Provide quality distribution to link up with midfield players and forwards, short passes, wall passes, driven passes, Long- lofted passes into space behind opponents. Provide quality crosses into the penalty area, as well as diagonal passes to change point of attack.

Width Length and Depth, Provide width length and depth by identifying and moving into spaces.
 Be always available to receive a pass; look to retain possession in midfield 1/3rd by controlling and shielding with back to goal, then link up with supporting midfield and forward players.
Create space by positioning and staying wide at every opportunity being available to receive the ball.
Look to take defenders on 1v 1with speed and pace, creating opportunities to deliver crosses into the penalty area , Time your runs and get on the end of crosses from the opposite side

Mobility, Provide good movement by checking away from opponents towards the ball in wide midfield areas, recognize and time diagonal runs in behind the defending line to exploit the space in behind.

Playing Roles and Responsibilities
In a 3-5-2 formation

- **Goalkeeper**

Refer to 4-4-2 presentation on page 22 as the roles of this player in a 3-5-2 formation are the same.

- **<u>Inside Right Midfield</u> Player in the 3-5-2 formation**

Refer to 4-3-3 presentation on page 39 as the roles of this player in the 3-5 -2 formation are similar.

- **<u>Central</u> Holding Midfield Player in the 3-5-2 formation**

Refer to 4-3-3 presentation on page 38 as the roles of this player in the 3-5-2 formation are similar.

- **<u>Inside Left</u> Midfield Player in the 3-5-2 formation**

Refer to 4-3-3 presentation on page 40 as the roles of this player in the 3-5-2 formation are similar.

- **<u>2 forwards</u> in the <u>midfield 1/3rd</u> in the 3-5-2 formation**

Refer to 4-4-2 presentation on page 31 as the roles of this player in the 3-5-2 formation are the same

- **<u>2 forwards</u> in the <u>attacking 1/3rd</u> in the 3-5-2 formation**

Refer to 4-4-2 presentation on page 32 as the roles of this player in the 3-5-2 formation are the same

Variation's on player organization
3 – 5 – 2 Formation
Flat Back 3 / Triangle Midfield 3 / 2 Wingers

Goalkeeper	Defending Unit Flat Back 4	Midfield Unit Triangle 3 / 2 Wingers	2 Strikers
1	1 Right defender 1 Central defenders 1 Left defender	1 Outside right winger 1 Central Midfield (Holding) 1 Right Midfield 1 Left Midfield 1 Outside left winger	1 left 1 right

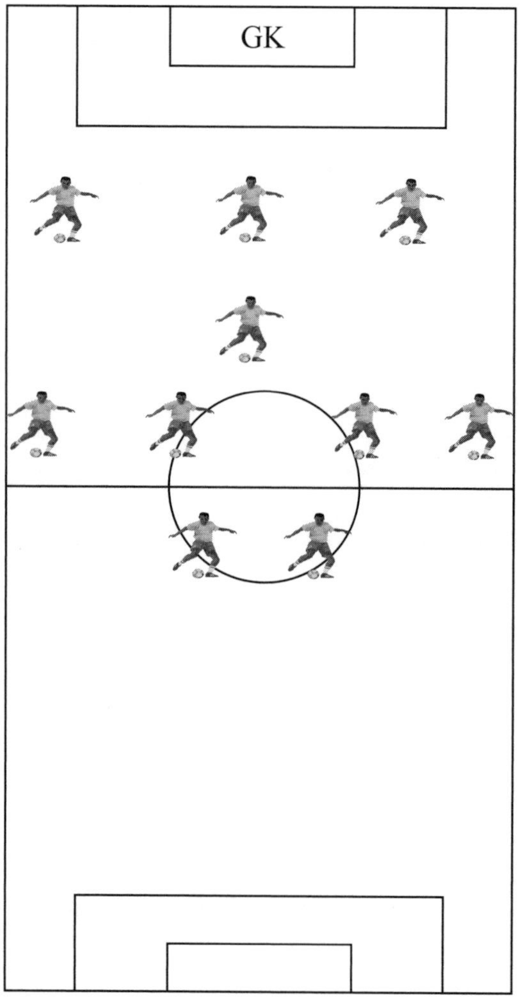

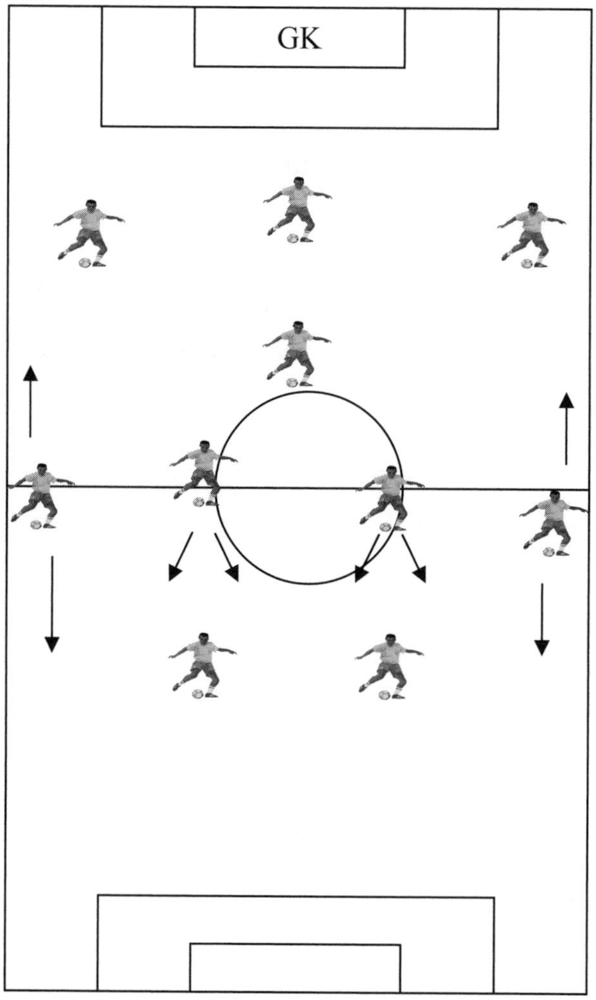

TEAM SHAPE WHEN DEFENDING   **TEAM SHAPE WHEN ATTACKING**

←——————→

TRANSITION

Compact position in relation to where the ball moves   Provide length width, and depth to create space

Formation is adaptable and flexible in attack transitioning from a 3-5-2 to a 3-4-3

58

Variation's on player organization
3 – 5 – 2 Formation
Flat Back 3 / Triangle Midfield 3 / 2 Wingers

Goalkeeper	Defending Unit Flat Back 3	Midfield Unit Triangle 3 / 2 Wingers	2 Strikers
1	1 Right defender 1 Central defenders 1 Left defender	1 Outside right winger 2 Central Midfield (Holding) 1 Central Midfield (Attacking) 1 Left Midfield 1 Outside left winger	1 left 1 right

TEAM SHAPE WHEN DEFENDING　　　**TEAM SHAPE WHEN ATTACKING**

TRANSITION

Compact position in relation to where the ball moves　　　Provide length width, and depth to create space
Formation is adaptable and flexible in attack transitioning from a 3-5-2 to a 3-4-3

Chapter 7
Functional Training Activities

Goalkeepers

Functional Training Activities Goalkeeper
"Receiving and Distribution"

Warm up:

Organization

- 2 Goalkeepers or 1 goalkeeper and a coach stand 5/10 yards apart
- Throw the ball forwards and backwards to each other at various heights.
- Deal with the ball along the ground , around your waist , above your head
- Distribution, under arm throw, over arm throws, sideways to throw.

Activity 1:

Organization

- 1 goal , 1 goalkeeper , 1 servers , Area 18 yard box
- Server plays the ball to goalkeeper who catches the ball then distributes out to other server, Repeat Exercise. Quality on the Service

Variations:
- Server plays the ball in along the ground
- Server plays the ball in at waist height.
- Server plays the ball in above head height

Activity 2:

Organization

- 1 goal , 1 goalkeeper , 2 servers , Area 18 yard box
- Server plays the ball to goalkeeper who catches the ball then distributes out to target player, to change the point of attack
- Distribution with hands – feet to target player
- Repeat Exercise. Quality on the Service

Variations:
- Server plays the ball in along the ground
- Server plays the ball in at waist height.
- Server plays the ball in above head height

Coaching Points

- Correct Technique when ball is above your head – Hands in "W" formation
- Correct Technique when ball is around your waist – Hands in the Bucket formation
- Correct Technique when ball is around your feet – hands in scoop formation
- Timing and positioning getting in line of flight of the ball – Move your feet.
- Make the correct decision which technique to use ,

Functional Training Activities Goalkeeper
"Dealing with Shots"

Activity 1

Organization
• 2 Goalkeepers or 1 goalkeeper and a coach stand 5/10 yards apart in front of 2 goals
• Area goal-box
• Throw the ball forwards and backwards to each other at various heights.
• Deal with the ball along the ground , around your waist , above your head
• Distribution, under arm throw, over arm throws, sideways to throw.

Activity 2

Organization
• 2 players , 1 goalkeeper
• 1 is goalkeeper in goal - 2 serving
• Area goal-box
• Good supply of balls
• Servers take in turn shooting at the goalkeeper; Goalkeeper must react to the ball being played in.

Coaching points to observe

- Correct Technique when ball is above your head – Hands in "W" formation
- Correct Technique when ball is around your waist – Hands in the Bucket formation
- Correct Technique when ball is around your feet – when receiving look to scoop under the ball
- Be alive and alert
- React to the delivery , speed , height , angle of the ball
- Make an early decision which technique to use.
- Distance and angles in relation to the goal posts and position of the ball.

Functional Training Activities Goalkeeper
"Dealing with crosses from wide area's"

Activity 1

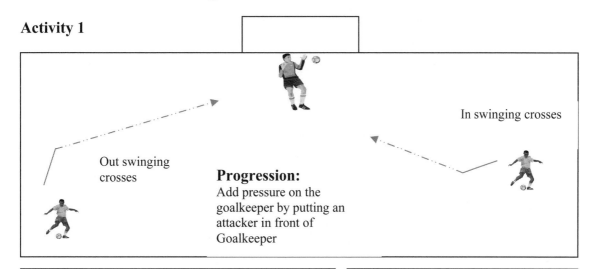

In swinging crosses

Out swinging crosses

Progression:
Add pressure on the goalkeeper by putting an attacker in front of Goalkeeper

Coaching points	Organization
• Be alive and alert • React to the delivery , speed , height of the ball • In swinging crosses – Out swinging crosses • Make an early decision which technique to use. • Distance and angles in relation to the goal posts and position of the ball. • Dealing with other players in your box PRESSURE	• 1 Goalkeeper • 2 wide players • Good supply of balls • Players in wide positions cross the ball into the box for the goalkeeper to deal with. Vary the service

Activity 2

Organization
- Area 36 x 60 wide 2 goals , good supply of balls
- 2 goalkeepers , 2 v 2 / 3 v 3 in the middle, 2 wide neutral players in channels out wide
- Goalkeeper starts by playing the ball wide. Wide players vary crosses into the box.
- **Coaching points**: As Above

Game Related Activity Goalkeeper

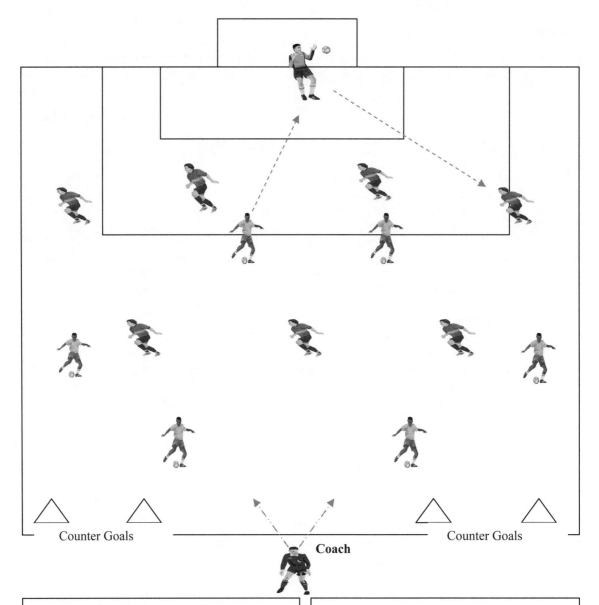

Counter Goals

Counter Goals

Coach

Organization	Coaching points

• Play on half the field
• Defending team – 8 players 1 goalkeeper, either a back 3 or 4, Midfield 3 or 4.
• Attacking team 6 players –
  2 forward players 4 midfield players
• Attacking Team goes to goal
• Defending team goes to counter goals
• Coach serves the ball in from half way
	• Goalkeepers position in relation to the ball
	• Communication
	  Provide good information to defenders.
	• Technique
	• Decision Making
	• Distribution

Chapter 8

Functional Training Activities

Defenders

Functional Training Defenders
Defending Activities

Activity 1 - 1 v 1

Organization:

- Area 15 x 10
- 2 Teams 2 players in each team
- Good supply of soccer balls
- Coach alternates serving the ball to each team.
- Defending player closes down quickly
- Attacking player has to dribble the ball across the end line between the cones
- If the defender wins the ball, in transition they can score across their opponent's line between the 2 cones.

Activity 2 - 2 v 1 then 2 v 2

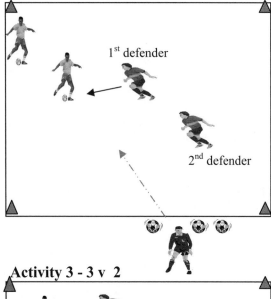

Organization

- Area 20 x 10 or appropriate sized for ability of players.
- 2 teams of 3 or 4 players
- Good supply of soccer balls
- Coach alternates the service to each team.
- 1st defender (player closest to the ball) closes down quickly.
- 2nd defender provides support to the 1st defender
- Attacking team has to run the ball between the cones
- If the defender wins the ball, in transition they can score across their opponent's line between the 2 cones.

Activity 3 - 3 v 2

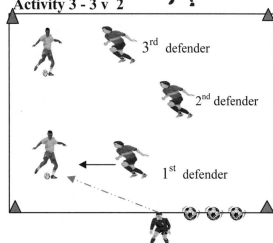

Organization

- Area 35 x 20 or appropriate sized for ability of players. 2 teams of 3 or 4 players
- Good supply of soccer balls
- Coach alternates the service to each team.
- 1st defender (player closest to the ball) closes down quickly.
- 2nd defender provides support to the 1st defender
- 3rd defender provides balance
- Attacking team has to run the ball between the cones
- If the defender wins the ball, in transition they can score across their opponent's line between the 2 cones.

Functional Training Phase of Play
Defending Activities

Activity 1   **2 v 2 to goal**

Coach starts game

Activity 2   **Phase of Play 5 v 4 to goal**

Coach starts game

Organization:

- Area Half Field
- 2 Teams
- 1 Goalkeeper 2 Defenders, 2 attacking players in each zone play 2v2 to goal
- Good supply of soccer balls.
- Attacking team of 2 players go to goal
- Defending team score through the counter goals, or play to the coach.
- Coach serves into wide attacking players.
- Observe the tendencies of the 1st defender
- Observe the positioning of the 2nd defender

Coaching Points

- Shape behind the ball in relation to position of the ball
- Marking responsibilities, Communication Zonal Defending , Man to Man,
- Tracking runs of attacking players
- Tackling and winning possession of the ball

Organization:

- Area Half Field
- 2 Teams
- 1 Goalkeeper 5 Defenders, 4 attacking players
- Good supply of soccer balls.
- Attacking team of 4 players go to goal
- Defending team score through the counter goals.
- Offside Rule is in play
- Coach serves into wide attacking players.
- Observe the tendencies of the 1st defender
- Observe the positioning of the 2nd defender
- Observe the position of the 3rd balancing defender

Functional Training Activities Defenders
Tackling and winning possession of the ball

Activity 1 Block tackles 50 / 50 challenges   **Organization:**

Organization
- Area 5 x 5 , 2 players 1 ball between 2
- The 2 players are stationary, on the coaches command they come together and perform a block tackle.

Coaching points
- Timing ,
- Good Body shape, . Body weight forward
- Ankle locked , inside of the foot to tackle,
- Body weight forward
- Be committed when you make your decision to tackle

Activity 2 Tackling when a player is running at them

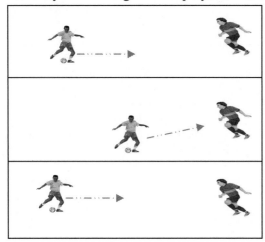

Organization
- Area 20 x 10 or appropriate sized for ability of players.
- Attacking player runs at the defender
- Defender attempts to win the ball and pass across line at the back of the area

Coaching Points
- Delay attacker with the ball
- Good body shape
- Stay on your feet
- Timing of your tackle
- Mentally, be a presence, Don't get beat.

Activity 3   Tackling when ball is running away from players

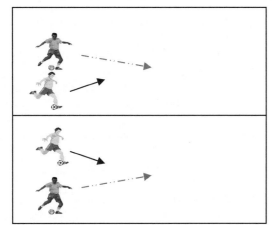

Players run with the ball ----·---►
Players run without the ball ———►

Organization
- Area 20 x 10 or appropriate sized for ability of players.
- 2 players start side by side
- The ball is played into space for the 2 players to run onto.
- White defending player tries to get to the ball 1st if not slide to try and win the ball

Coaching Points
- Speed and pace, get to the ball first
- Good body shape
- Stay on your feet
- Timing of your tackle
- Last resort Sliding Tackle.
- Mentally , Be a presence , Don't get beat.

Functional Training Activities Defenders
Defending heading dealing with the ball in the air

Activity 1

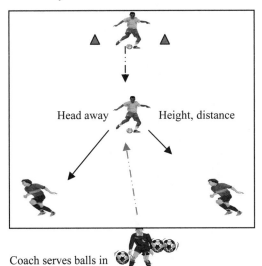

Head away   Height, distance

Coach serves balls in

Organization

- Area 15 x 10
- Good supply of soccer balls
- Coach alternates serving the ball to each player in the air
- Player starts in between the cones. Player moves forward to attack the ball played in the air
- Coach alternates height of the serve
- Clear the ball with height and length to the 2 target players

  Rotate after each one , person who heads become the target player .

Activity 2

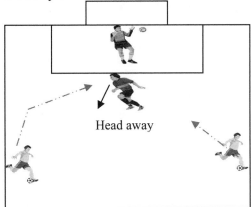

Head away

Progress by adding an attacker

Organization

- Area 18 yard box
- Good supply of balls
- 2 servers out wide serving, One on the right side, One on the left side, Cross the ball in at various heights.
- 1 goalkeeper (who communicates to defender)
- Start with one defender in their specific position, on the edge of the 18yrd box , defending crosses
- Add defenders to create either a back 3 or back 4
- Add opposition 1 player at a time.

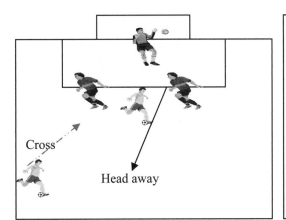

Cross

Head away

Coaching Points

- Communication - call your name
- Getting your body into line, Flight of the ball
- Timing and judging the speed , height and pace of the ball
- Use your upper body and fore head to attack the ball, keeping you eyes open.
- Follow the direction of the ball once you have headed away.
- Covering Defender also runs out in the direction of the ball

Chapter 9
Functional Training Activities

Midfielders

Functional Training Midfield Players
Passing for Penetration activities

Activity 1   Passing and Receiving

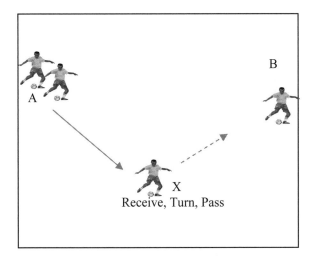

Receive, Turn, Pass

Organization
- Area 15 x 20 lengthen for longer range exercises
- Split into groups of 4
- Player A pass into player X who receives the ball turns and passes to player B
- Player X follows there pass to outside of grid to Player B
- Player A then moves from outside the grid into the middle to receive a pass from player B
- Variation: Pass in – man on – Pass out
  Pass in – Spin off – Get return

Activity 2 Passing and Receiving

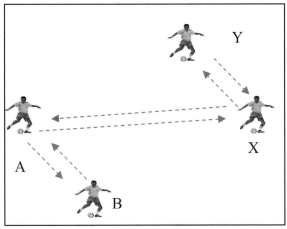

Organization
- Area 20 x 30 or appropriate sized for ability of players.
- Sequence: X pass to Y
  Y pass to X
  X passes across to A
  A pass to B
  B pass to A
  A passes across area to X

Repeat Sequence
Variation : 2 touch – 1 touch – combination
  Interchange positions

Coaching Points
- **Accuracy on passing**
- **Correct weight of the pass**
- **Pass with the correct surface of the foot**

Functional Training Midfield Players
Game Related Activity

Activity 1

Switch the play

Organization

- Area 35 x 20 or appropriate sized for ability of players.
- 3 v 3 or 4 v 4 with 4 neutral target players on the outside of the area
- Score by playing into target players
- When a target players receive the ball play across to other target player to start the game again.
  Change point of attack
  Rotate players in the Middle

Coaching Points

Switch the play

Activity 2   **6 v 6 four goal game**

2 teams play 6 v 6 score by either passing or dribbling through any goal can not score in the same goal in succession.

Functional Training Defenders / Midfield players
Passing to space on the Run

Activity 1

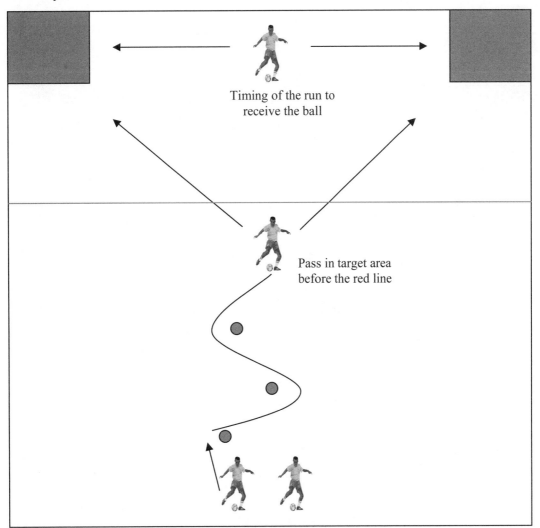

Timing of the run to
receive the ball

Pass in target area
before the red line

Organization

1. Area 40 long 30 wide
2. 2 target boxes 10 yards each in corners
4. Target player stands in between, the 2 Red target boxes
5. Player with the ball dribbles around cones then before the ball crosses the mid line pass the ball into either target box.
6. Player who passes the ball becomes the target player.
7. Target Player runs onto the pass in the box.

Coaching Points:
1. Good Control with ball at your feet, Keep head up, Vision
2. Use the inside/outside of the foot to pass the ball
3. Good speed ,weight and accuracy on your pass
4. The target player times there run onto the pass

Functional Training Defenders / Midfield players
Passing to space on the Run

Activity 2

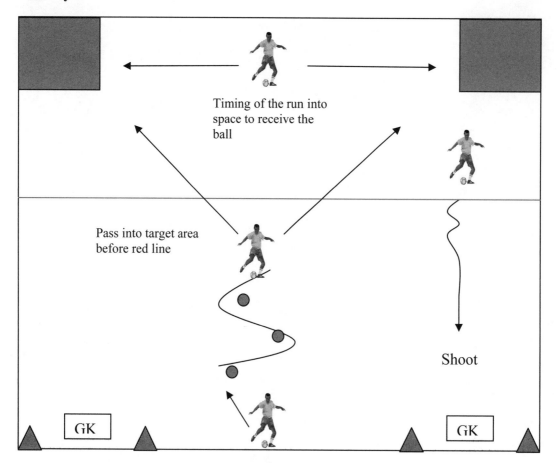

Timing of the run into space to receive the ball

Pass into target area before red line

Shoot

GK

GK

Organization

1. Area 40 long 30 wide
2. 2 target boxes 10 yards each in corners
4. Target player stands in between, the 2 Red target boxes
5. Player with the ball dribbles around cones then before the ball crosses the mid line pass the ball into either target box.
6. Player who passes the ball becomes the target player.
7. Target player runs onto the pass in the box.
8. When they receive the pass they break out and try to score on a goalkeeper.

Coaching Points:
1. Good Control with ball at your feet, Keep head up , vision
2. Use the inside of the foot to pass the ball
3. Good speed ,weight and accuracy on your pass
4. The target player times there run onto the pass

Functional Small Sided Game Defenders / Midfield
Passing to Feet

Activity 1

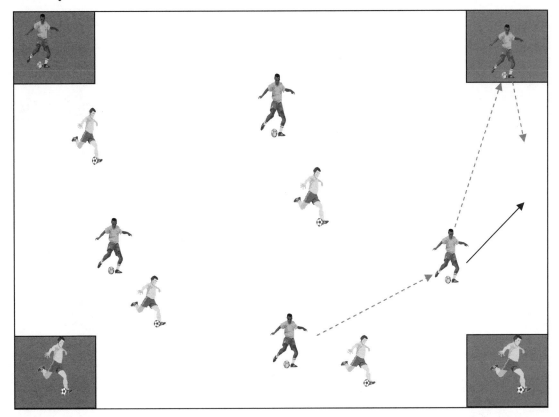

Organization
Organization
Passing on the run to feet to targets
1. Area 40 long 30 wide
2. 4 target players in corner boxes 10 x 10 yards
4. Play 4 v 4 in the middle
5. Score by playing the ball into Target players , cant score in the same corner in succession, Although you can play back to the same target as a support pass to retain possession.
6. Progressions, Unlimited touch, 3 touch, 2 touch, 1 touch
Target players 2 touch, or 1 touch.
7. Change Target Player
Coaching Points:
• Good control with ball at your feet, keep head up , Vision
• Use the inside / outside of the foot to pass the ball
• Good speed ,weight and accuracy on your pass
• Movement of the ball

Activity 2

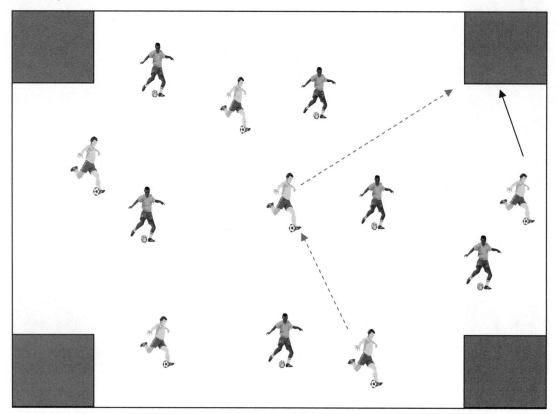

Organization
Passing to Space

1. Area 60 long 40 wide
2. Corner boxes 10 x 10 yards
4. Play 6 v 6 or 8 v 8 in the middle
5. Score by playing the ball into the corner.
Player cannot stand in the box to receive, they must time there run into the box
Cannot score in the same corner in succession,
6. Progressions, Unlimited touch, 3 touch, 2 touch, 1 touch

Coaching Points:
- Good control with ball at your feet, keep head up , Vision
- Use the inside / outside of the foot to pass the ball
- Good speed ,weight and accuracy on your pass
- Movement of the ball, Timing of runs into corner

Functional Training Midfield and Strikers
Crossing and Finishing

Activity 1 Front post runs

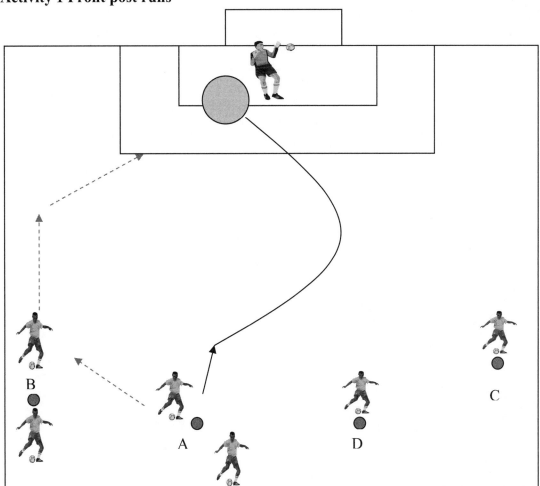

Organization

1. Area 40 long 75 wide
2. 1 goal 8 yards wide, 1 Goalkeeper in the goal.
3. Good supply of soccer balls
4. 2 players stand out wide in gate B, players stand at cones A in the middle
5. To Start Player A passes out wide into space for player B to run onto, Player A then runs away from the ball , then checks back and attacks the near / Front post area of the 18 yard box,
6. Player B delivers the ball to the near post , Player A attempts to Score.

To play on the opposite side, repeat exercise but start in positions D and C.

Coaching Points :

Quality on the passing,

Correct weight and accuracy of the pass either to feet or space.

Correct timing of the runs both on the ball and off the ball

Quality delivery of the ball on crosses into the near post area

Finish your chances

Functional Training Midfield and Strikers
Crossing and Finishing

Activity 2 Front post runs
Progression

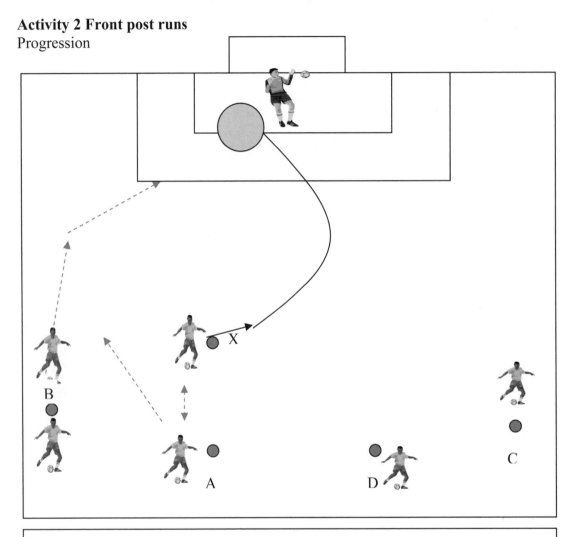

Organization

1. Area 40 long 75 wide
2. 1 goal 8 yards wide, 1 Goalkeeper in the goal.
3. Good supply of soccer balls
4. 2 players stand out wide in gates B, players stand at cones A and X in the middle
5. To Start Player A passes inside to player X, Player X lays the ball back for Player A who passes out wide into space for player B to run onto, Player X then runs away from the ball, then checks back and attacks the near / Front post area of the 18 yard box, Once Player A passes wide they take up position X. The same organization on opposite side.
6. Player B delivers the ball to the near post , Player X attempts to Score.
7. To play on the opposite side , Start in positions D , Y , C

Coaching Points:
Quality on the passing, speed of play 1 and 2 touch combination play
Correct weight and accuracy of the pass either to feet or space.
Correct timing of the runs both on the ball and off the ball
Quality delivery of the ball on crosses into the near post area
Finish your chances

Functional Training Midfield and Strikers
Crossing and Finishing

Activity 1 Far post runs

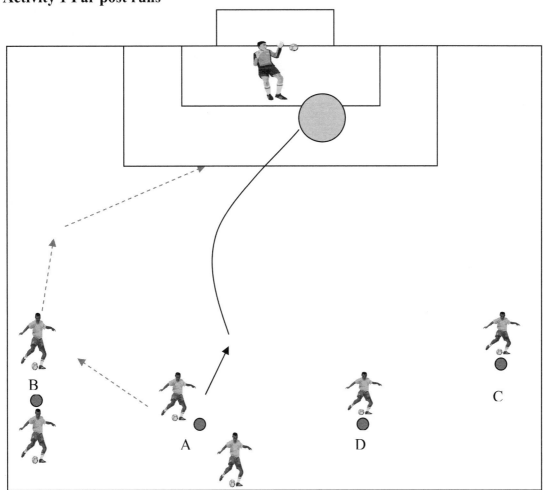

Organization

1. Area 40 long 70 wide
2. 1 goal 8 yards wide, 1 Goalkeeper in the goal.
3. Good supply of soccer balls
4. 2 players stand out wide in gate B, players stand at cones A in the middle
5. To Start Player A passes out wide into space for player B to run onto, Player A then runs towards the ball , then runs away and attacks the far / back post area of the 18 yard box,
6. Player B delivers the ball to the far post, Player A attempts to Score.
To play on the opposite side, repeat exercise but start in positions D and C

Coaching Points:
Quality on the passing,
Correct weight and accuracy of the pass either to feet or space.
Correct timing of the runs both on the ball and off the ball
Quality delivery of the ball on crosses into the near post area
Finish your chances, on the ground and in the air

Functional Training Midfield and Strikers
Crossing and Finishing

Activity 2 Far post runs

Progression

Organization

1. Area 40 long 70 wide
2. 1 goal 8 yards wide , 1 Goalkeeper in the goal.
3. Good supply of soccer balls
4. 2 players stand out wide in gates B, players stand at cones A and X in the middle
5. To Start Player A passes inside to player X, Player X lays the ball back for Player A who passes out wide into space for player B to run onto, Player X then runs towards the ball , then attacks the Far post area of the 18 yard box, Once Player A passes wide they take up position X . The same organization on opposite side .
6. Player B delivers the ball to the far post , Player X attempts to Score.
7. To play on the opposite side , Start in positions D , Y , C

Coaching Points

Quality on the passing, Speed of play 1 and 2 touch combination play

Correct weight and accuracy of the pass either to feet or space.

Correct timing of the runs both on the ball and off the ball

Quality delivery of the ball on crosses into the near post area

Finish your chances, on the ground and in the air

Functional Training Midfield and Strikers
Crossing and Finishing from the touchline

Activity 1
Crossing and finishing at front post

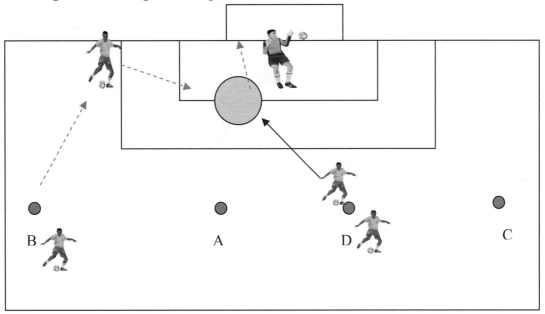

Organization
1. Area 40 long 70 wide
2. 1 goal 8 yards wide , 1 Goalkeeper in the goal.
3. Good supply of soccer balls
4. 2 players stand out wide in gate B, players stand at cones A in the middle
5. To Start Player B dribbles and attacks the end line in the 18 yard box,
6. Player B then cuts (passes) the ball back to towards the penalty spot / near post area along the ground.
7. Player D then runs diagonally onto the pass towards the near post and attempts to score. Option Players can run from position A
Play then on the opposite side, players start in position A and C
Coaching Points

Coaching Points
Quality on the passing,
Correct weight and accuracy of the pass either to feet or space.
Correct timing of the runs both on the ball and off the ball
Quality delivery of the ball on crosses into the near post area
Finish your chances, on the ground and in the air

Functional Training Midfield and Strikers
Crossing and Finishing from the touchline

Activity 2
Crossing and finishing at the far post

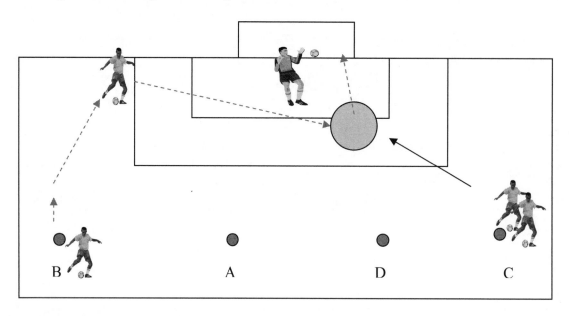

Organization

1. Area 40 long 70 wide
2. 1 goal 8 yards wide , 1 Goalkeeper in the goal.
3. Good supply of soccer balls
4. 2 players stand out wide in gates B, players stand at cones A and X in the middle
5. To Start Player B dribbles and attacks the end line in the 18 yard box,
6. Player B then Chips (passes) the ball back to towards the back post in the air
7. Player C then runs diagonally onto the pass towards the back post and attempts to score.
Option Players can run from position D
Play then on the opposite side, players start in position B and C

Coaching Points
Quality on the passing,
Correct weight and accuracy of the pass either to feet or space.
Correct timing of the runs both on the ball and off the ball
Quality delivery of the ball on crosses into the near post area
Finish your chances, on the ground and in the air

Functional Training for Midfield and Strikers
Crossing and Finishing Front and Back Post

Activity 1

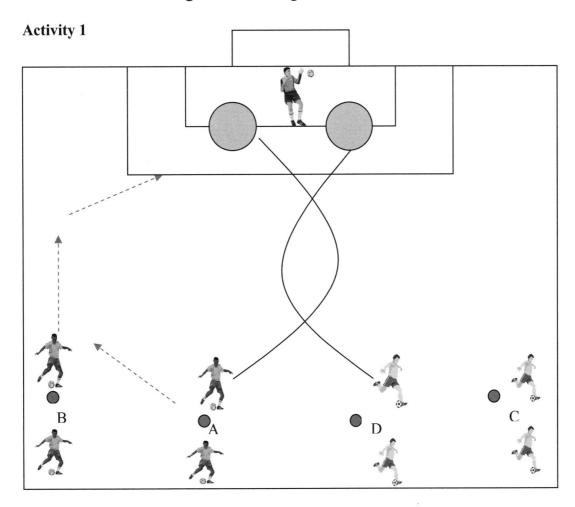

Organization

1. Area 40 long 70 wide
2. 1 goal 8 yards wide , 1 Goalkeeper in the goal.
3. Good supply of soccer balls
4. 2 players stand out wide in gate B, 2 groups of players stand at cones A and D in the middle
5. To Start Player A passes out wide into space for player B to run onto, Player A then runs away from the ball , then checks back and attacks the near / front post area of the 18 yard box,
Player D runs towards the ball then checks away and positions themselves at the back post .
6. Player B delivers the ball to either the near post or far post Area, Players A and D attempt to Score.
Play then the opposite side and repeat exercise
Coaching Points:
Quality on the passing.
Correct weight and accuracy of the pass either to feet or space.
Correct timing of the runs both on the ball and off the ball into the penalty area
Quality delivery of the ball on crosses into the near post area
Finish your chances, on the ground and in the air
Communication

Functional Training for Midfield and Strikers
Crossing and Finishing Front and Back Post

Activity 2
Progression

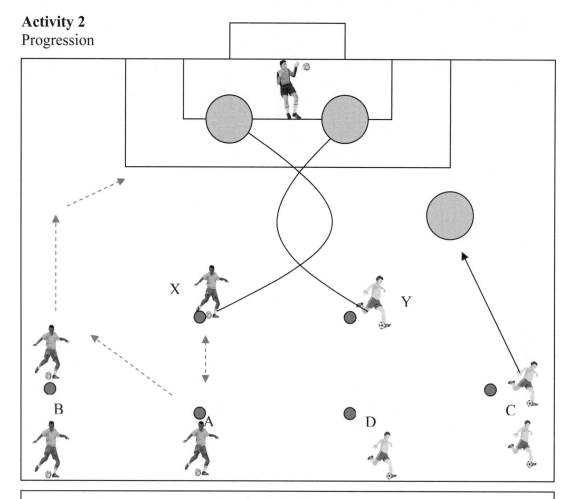

Organization

Area 40 long 70 wide
1. 1 goal 8 yards wide , 1 Goalkeeper in the goal.
2. Good supply of soccer balls
3. 2 players stand out wide in gates B and C , 2 groups of players stand at cones D and C in the middle
4. To Start Player A passes inside to player X, Player X lays the ball back for Player A who Passes out wide into space for player B to run onto, Player X then runs away from the ball , then checks back and attacks the near / Front post area of the 18 yard box, , Player Y runs towards the ball then checks away and positions themselves at the back post .
5. Once Player A passes wide they take up position X ..
6. Player B delivers the ball to the near post , Player X , Y attempts to Score.
7. Player C joins in around the back . Play then the opposite side ,

Coaching Points:
Quality on the passing, Speed of play, 1 and 2 touch, combination play
Correct weight and accuracy of the pass either to feet or space.
Correct timing of the runs both on the ball and off the ball into the penalty area
Quality delivery of the ball on crosses into the near post area
Finish your chances, on the ground and in the air
Communication

Functional Training for Midfield and Strikers
Crossing and Finishing
Front, Back Post and Edge of the box

Activity 1

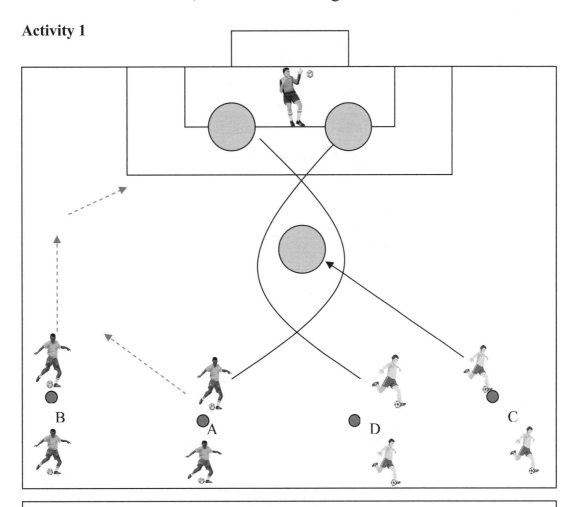

Organization
1. Area 40 long 70 wide
2. 1 goal 8 yards wide , 1 Goalkeeper in the goal.
3. Good supply of soccer balls
4. 2 players stand out wide in gate B, 2 groups of players stand at cones A and D in the middle
5. To Start Player A passes out wide into space for player B to run onto, Player A then runs away from the ball , then checks back and attacks the near / Front post area of the 18 yrd box, Player D runs towards the ball then checks away and positions themselves at the back post .
6. Player B delivers the ball to either the near post or far post Area, Players A and D attempt to Score. Player C runs inside and looks for a shot on the edge of the box
Play then the opposite side and repeat exercise
Coaching Points:
Quality on the passing.
Correct weight and accuracy of the pass either to feet or space.
Correct timing of the runs both on the ball and off the ball into the penalty area
Quality delivery of the ball on crosses into the near post area
Finish your chances, on the ground and in the air
Communication

Functional Training for Midfield and Strikers
Crossing and Finishing
Front, Back Post and Edge of the box

Activity 2

Progression overlapping run

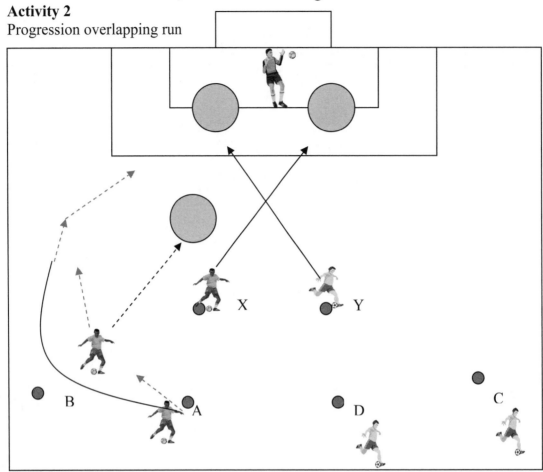

Organization

1. Area 40 long 70 wide
2. 1 goal 8 yards wide , 1 Goalkeeper in the goal.
3. Good supply of soccer balls
4. 2 players stand out wide in gates B and C , 2 groups of players stand at cones D and C in the middle
5. To Start Player A passes out wide to player B, Player A then follows there pass and <u>overlaps</u> Player B. Player B passes back into the run of player A.
6. Player A crosses the ball into the box
7. Player B continues there run and takes up a position on the edge of the box. Players X and Y organize there run's, Player X goes Back Post, Player Y runs near Post.
8. The same organization happens on opposite side.

   Coaching Points:

   Quality on the passing, Speed of play, 1 and 2 touch, combination play

   Correct weight and accuracy of the pass either to feet or space.

   Correct timing of the runs both on the ball and off the ball into the penalty area

   Quality delivery of the ball on crosses into the penalty area

   Finish your chances, on the ground and in the air

   Communication

Functional Training for Midfield and Strikers
Crossing and Finishing
Front, Back Post and Edge of the box

Activity 3
Progression give and go

Cross into the penalty box

X

Y

B

A

D

C

Organization

1. Area 40 long 70 wide
2. 1 goal 8 yards wide, 1 Goalkeeper in the goal.
3. Good supply of soccer balls
4. 2 players stand out wide in positions B and C , 2 groups of players stand at cones D and C in the middle
5. To Start Player B plays a <u>give and go</u> with Player X, Player X then turns, runs and takes up a position at the back post
6. Player Y runs near post
7. Player B crosses the ball into the box
8. Player A runs and takes up a position on the edge of the box.
9. The same organization happens on opposite side.

Coaching Points:
Quality on the passing, Speed of play, 1 and 2 touch, combination play
Correct weight and accuracy of the pass either to feet or space.
Correct timing of the runs both on the ball and off the ball into the penalty area
Quality delivery of the ball on crosses into the penalty area
Finish your chances, on the ground and in the air
Communication

Functional Training for Midfield and Strikers
Crossing and Finishing
Front, Back Post and Edge of the box

Activity 4
Diagonal Pass

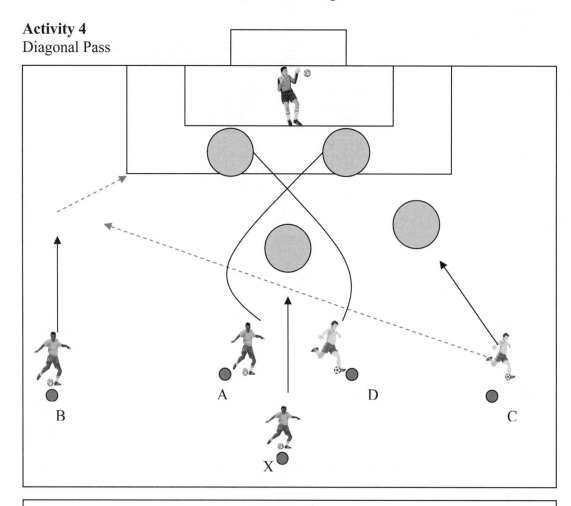

| | | B | | A | | D | | | C |

Organization

1. Area 40 long 70 wide
2. 1 goal 8 yards wide, 1 Goalkeeper in the goal.
3. Good supply of soccer balls
4. 2 players stand out wide in gate B and C, 2 groups of players stand at cones A and D in the middle
5. To Start Player C passes a Diagonal cross field ball into space for player B to run onto, Player C then runs towards the back post area,
Player A and D organize there runs front and back post
6. Player B delivers the ball to either the near post or far post Area, Players A and D attempt to Score. Player C looks for a shot on the edge of the box.
Player X delays there run and takes up a position just outside the 18yrd box.
Play then the opposite side and repeat exercise
Option Player X can play the ball out to Player C
Coaching points : as activity 3

Chapter 10
Functional Training Activities

Forwards

Functional Training Forwards
Shooting in and around the penalty box

Activity 1

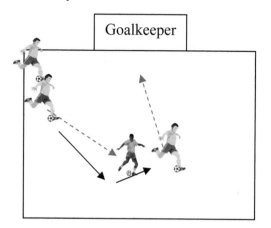

Goalkeeper

Organization
- Area 18 yard box goal
- Players on both sides of the goal
- Pass into coach who is standing 10 yard's away
- Coach lays the ball off
- Player goes around the coach and shoots on the Goalkeeper.
  ### Coaching Points
- Strike ball with laces, inside of foot
- Kick through the middle of the ball,
- Disguise your shot, Vision , knowledge of

Activity 2

Goalkeeper

Goalkeeper

Organization
- Area 2 x 18 yard box
- 2 goal 8 yards wide
- Good supply of soccer balls
- 2 teams, 2 goalkeeper,
- Play the ball out of your feet; shoot before the ball crosses line.
- Breakaways on the goalie run / Dribble and Shoot, then rotate around.
- Shoot with left foot / right foot
  ### Coaching Points
- Strike ball with instep laces, inside of foot
- Kick through the middle of the ball,
- Disguise your shot,
- Vision, knowledge of Goalkeeper's position.
- Finish rebound opportunities

Activity 3

Goalkeeper

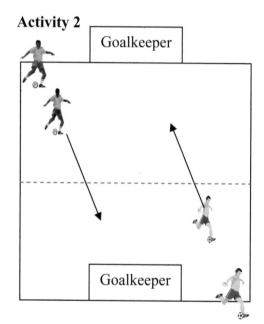

Shoot

2. Over-lap

1.Give and go

Organization
- Area Goal and 18 yard box
- Good supply of soccer balls
- 1 goalkeeper
- 1st attacking Player Plays a give and go, then shoots
- Variation:
  Over-lap and shoot
  Volley on the return pass
- Shoot with right foot / left foot
  Coaching Points:
  As Above

Functional Training
Forwards 1 touch / 2 touch finishing

Activity 4

Goalkeeper

Organization

- Area 18 yard box goal
- Good Supply of Soccer Balls
- Server lays the ball off to the right side
- Player Shoots with there right foot
- Player then comes back around the server , Server lays the ball off to the left side
- Player shoots with there left foot.
- Variations:
  Server can throw ball in the air for player to volley

Activity 5

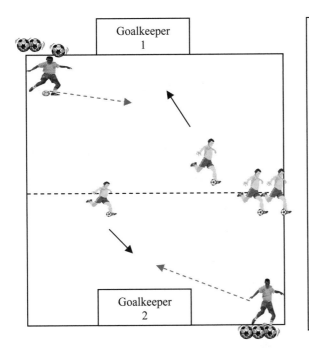

Goalkeeper 1

Goalkeeper 2

Organization
- Area 1 x 18 yard box
- 1 goal 8 yards wide
- Good supply of soccer balls
- Coach / Player crosses the ball in the air
- Striker / Forward times there run and head to score.
  Once the player attacks goalkeeper 1 they turn organize there runs and attack the 2nd goalkeeper.

Coaching Points
- Diagonal runs near and far post
- Timing of the runs
- Judging the flight of the ball
- Proper technique
- Decision making, head with power and accuracy or glancing header with placement and accuracy.

Functional Training Forwards

Activity 6

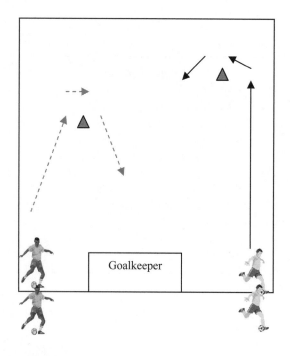

Organization

- Area 20 x 25
- 1 goal 8 yards wide
- Good supply of soccer balls
- 2 teams, 1 goalkeeper,1 team is the shooting team, the other team is the defending team.
- The shooting team has to dribble around cone # 1 which is 15 yards away and shoot at goal.
- The defender has to run around cone # 2 20yrds away.

Activity 7

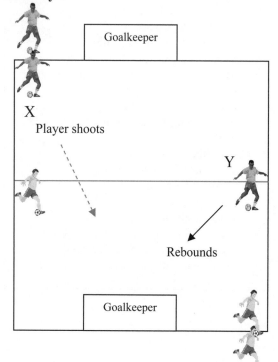

Organization
Rebound opportunities

- Area 20 x 25
- 2 goals 8yrds wide
- Good supply of soccer balls
- 2 goalkeepers
- Player X dribbles and shoots before the ball crosses the red line.
- Player Y starts on the red line
- As player X shoots player Y is reacting to the rebound if there is one.
- White team then play the opposite side
- Rotate the rebound players

Functional Training Forwards
Game Related Activity

Activity 8
2 v 2 + 2 neutral wide players to goal

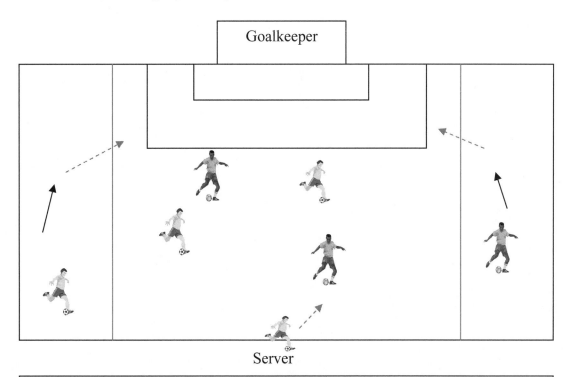

Organization

- Area 60 wide by 35, 1 goal
- Good supply of soccer balls
- 1 goalkeeper ,2 v 2 in the middle
- 2 neutral players in wide channels who serve crosses in the box.
- Server at the edge of the box plays the ball in
- White defending team if they win the ball play out to the server,
  Gold team attacks the goal.
  Rotate teams
  Coaching Points:
  Runs of forward player, near post, Far post
  Timing of the runs
  Delivery of the crosses
  Finishing

Activity 8
4 v 4 + 2 neutral wide players to 2 goals

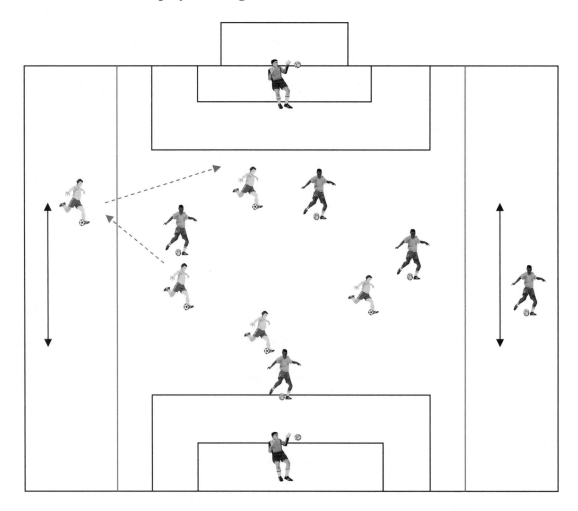

Organization

- Area 60 wide by 35, 1 goal
- Good supply of soccer balls
- 2 goalkeeper ,4 v 4 in the middle
- 2 neutral players in wide channels who serve crosses in the box.
  Rotate teams

  Coaching Points:
  Runs of forward players, near post, far post
  Timing of the runs
  Delivery of the crosses from wide positions
  Finishing, shoot at any opportunity

Glossary of terms

Awareness: A players understanding on the field of play in relation to the ball, opponents and teammates

Channeling : Directing the opposition player on the ball in a specific direction

Compact: In relation to team defensive organization distances between players should be closer together.

Creating Space: Movement off the ball to open up space to either receives the ball or a teammate to run into.

Far Post: This is the area of the goal that is the furthest way from the goalposts.

Functional Training Activity : Training the player in there specific position with activities that are appropriate to that position .

Jockeying: This is the term used for defenders to hold up the attacker from going forward with the ball .

Man to Man Marking: Staying with an opponent as they move around the field

Near Post: This is the area of the goal that is the closest to the player and the ball

Overlapping runs : Running around the outside of your teammate

Shielding: Protecting the ball by putting your body in between the ball and the opponent

System of play: Numbers of players in specific areas of the field.

Tracking: Following an opponent who is running off the ball

Vision: Recognizing what is happening in the game

Wall passes (give and go) Passing the ball to a teammate then getting a return pass back

Zonal defending: Marking space in your specific area of the field.

BOOKS

Item # 1022

The author shares his 20 years of experience coaching at pro youth academies in England.

This book shows some of the most creative, inspiring and innovative training sessions you will find anywhere.

$19.95

Item # 1019

This book takes an in-depth look at the formation used by Liverpool to win the Champions League Final.

Whether you play with a 4-4-2, 4-3-3, 3-4-3 or any other formation, understanding how to play the 3-5-2 formation is critical for any coach or team.

$24.95

Item # 1016

Contains 11 chapters showing practices and exercises used at English Premier League Academies to develop and improve technique. Chapters are: **Warm-Ups, Passing, Ball Control, Dribbling, Running, Shooting, Attacking Play, Defending, Tackling, Games and Tactics.**

$19.95

Item # 1007

Takes the exercises shown in Volume One and progresses them into functional sessions, then into tactical sessions and finally into game situations.

$19.95

Item # 1013

This incredible book shows every GOALKEEPER training session, practice and drill done by the New England Revolution from their 2002 season.

$24.95

Item # 1007

This one-of-a-kind book shows every training session, practice and drill of the Penn State soccer team from their 2001 season where they reached the NCAA Tournament round of 16.

$19.95

Item # 1011

This is the most comprehensive book ever written about the 4 - 4 - 2 formation. Covered are the roles and responsibilities of the defenders, midfielders and forwards in both attacking and defending situations.

$24.95

BEST SELLER!

Item # 1001

The most comprehensive book EVER published of soccer practices and training sessions. **Over 200 pages** full of training sessions from **Manchester United, Brazil National Team, PSV Eindhoven, Boca Juniors,** etc.

$29.95

1,000's ALREADY SOLD!

Item # 1014

Over 200 pages and 100 training sessions from the world's top teams like **Manchester United, Ajax, Liverpool, Juventus, PSV Eindhoven and São Paulo.** These, plus sessions from National teams from **Holland, Italy, USA** and others make this book a "must have" for any serious soccer coach.

$29.95

Item # 1002

Includes training sessions and drills from **Manchester United, U.S. Women's World Cup Team, Venice of Serie "A", Liverpool F.C., Bodens BK of Sweden, Brazilian Youth Teams** plus many of the MLS Teams and other top teams and coaches from around the world.

$12.95

Item # 1003

Includes training sessions and drills from **Manchester United, Juventus F.C. and Venice of Serie "A", Ajax F.C., Lausanne of Switzerland, Liverpool Academy** plus many of the MLS Teams and other top teams and coaches from around the world.

$12.95

Item # 1004

Includes training sessions and drills from **São Paulo of Brazil, Italy U15 National Team, Tony DiCicco, Liverpool F.C., Lira Lulea BK of Sweden, Leeds United** plus **New England Revolution of the MLS** and other top teams and coaches from around the world.

$12.95

Item # 1005

Includes training sessions and drills from **PSV Eindhoven, U.S. Women's World Cup Team, Ajax F.C., Liverpool F.C., Leeds United, FK Teplice** plus many of the MLS Teams and other top teams and coaches from around the world.

$12.95

Item # 1010

Included are 32 complete training sessions covering **passing, receiving, dribbling, running with the ball, shooting, defending and goalkeeping**. There are also 16 fun, small-sided games that can be used in any training session or as warm-ups.

$14.95

Item # 1008

Included are 32 complete training sessions covering **passing, receiving, dribbling, running with the ball, shooting, defending and goalkeeping**. There are also 22 fun, small-sided games that can be used in any training session or as warm-ups.

$14.95

To Order Call
1-888-342-6224

OR VISIT

WORLDCLASSCOACHING.COM